The Immigration Time Bomb

**G. Palmer Stacy III
and Wayne Lutton, Ph.D.**

The American Immigration Control Foundation
Alexandria, Virginia

Acknowledgements

The authors wish to express their thanks to the many men and women of the Immigration and Naturalization Service, Justice Department, State Department, Social Security Administration and Congressional staffs, who generously shared their knowledge and experiences with us. We also note our appreciation to the following individuals for the valuable advice they gave us on various parts of this book: Dr. Arthur Corwin, former consultant to the House Immigration Subcommittee; Dr. Samuel Francis, specialist in problems of terrorism and national security; and Mr. Lee Edwards, for his assistance in the area of documentation fraud.

Dedication

Dedicated to the generous Patriots who support the American Immigration Control Foundation. Without their help, this book and the work of AICF would not be possible.

TABLE OF CONTENTS

INTRODUCTION

The Immigration Time Bomb

America is being invaded.

Every day thousands of foreigners illegally enter our country. Over two million illegal aliens will come this year, most of them penetrating our porous 2,000-mile border with Mexico. Additional hundreds of thousands will arrive through our superficially inspected harbors and international airports. In 1975, General Leonard Chapman, Commissioner of the Immigration and Naturalization Service (INS) warned: "Illegal immigration is out of control."

The total number of illegal aliens already in the United States may exceed 12 million -- more than twice the size of the Soviet armed forces.

President Ronald Reagan stated on October 19, 1983, that "This country has lost control of its own borders, and no country can sustain that kind of position."

Most illegal aliens come to the United States looking for work and end up displacing American citizens from what are often well-paying jobs. Others are lured by our burgeoning welfare state, and are assisted by "religious" and "welfare rights" groups to obtain benefits intended for needy Americans and paid for by over-burdened U.S. taxpayers. Still other aliens are heavily involved in crime and welfare fraud, while some engage in terrorism and subversion.

Several major cities have already been turned into extensions of foreign countries, where English is not spoken and Americans are not welcome. Aliens threaten to seize political power within a few short years in a number of states, including California, New Mexico, Texas and Florida. Leading figures on both sides of the Mexican border speak openly and approvingly about ''reconquering'' the southwestern United States from the despised ''Anglos.''

When concerned American citizens ask their leaders to halt this invasion, they are told that nothing can be done and that, after all, ''this is a nation of immigrants.''

These sentimental imageries (''Give me your tired, your poor . . . .'') have been used to blind many Americans to the dangers presented by uncontrolled immigration. Our security as a nation, our economic prosperity, our domestic political unity and our standing in international affairs are being threatened as never before. A Georgetown University study concludes:

> Current U.S. immigration policy is a national disgrace. The beneficiaries of this policy remain politically powerful, unwilling to put aside narrow, special interests for the national good.

This vitally important book looks at the immigration time bomb planted in the heart of America; a bomb which comes closer to detonating every day. Unless we -- the American citizens and our elected representatives -- disarm this bomb, it will explode and destroy the United States we know and love.

Gordon J. MacDonald, Deputy Chief
U.S. Border Patrol, Retired

CHAPTER 1

A History of Immigration to the United States

In 1607 the first permanent English settlement in America was established at Jamestown, Virginia. In 1620 the English Pilgrims landed at Plymouth, Massachusetts. These hardy settler families were soon joined by many others. Despite frightful losses due to disease, starvation, and Indian attacks, the North American colonies had about 25,000 people by 1640. Their resourcefulness and industriousness, working in a continent incredibly rich in natural resources (and sparsely occupied by primitive "Indians"), led to a rapid increase in population. By 1741 the population of the colonies had reached nearly a million. Benjamin Franklin reportedly said that only 80,000 immigrants had multiplied to produce that population. Even if Franklin's estimate of total immigration was too low, the natural increase was remarkable.

By 1776, the year of American independence, the population was around 2,500,000. With the exception of black slaves and Indians, who played no role in government, the population was overwhelmingly composed of people of British descent. This fact was reflected in the backgrounds of the national leaders who signed the Declaration of Independence: all were English, Scotch, Welsh, or Irish. When the Constitutional Convention met in 1787, its members were all of British descent, except for a few of Dutch or mixed French-British ancestry.

In 1790, the first official census found a population of four million, including approximately 750,000 slaves. The ethnic background of the white population was as follows:

English	82.1%
Scotch	7.0%
German	5.6%
Dutch	2.5%
Irish	1.9%
French	.6%
Other	.3%

The freedoms brought by the settlers from England were defended and expanded in their New World home and formed the basis for our free, representative government. The other settlers, largely from Germany, the Netherlands, and other Northern European nations, gradually abandoned their native tongues and adopted English. The Spanish and French outposts in North America had little lasting impact on the U.S., although a few areas retained portions of their Spanish and French cultures. Contrary to the modern "melting pot" myth, which asserts that our nation was created out of a hodge-podge of ethnic groups and cultures, it was a homogeneous people who laid the foundation upon which our Republic rests.

The demand for pioneers to fill an empty and bountiful continent coincided with economic changes and overpopulation in Europe. Rapid population increase, the growth of industry and the breakup of the traditional agricultural order led hundreds of thousands of people from Northern and Western Europe to search for a new life. So the immigrants continued to come at an accelerating rate, although the numbers were still not large by comparison with the influx of later years. Only 8,385 immigrants arrived in 1820; but by 1840 annual immigration had reached 84,066.

The United Kingdom, Germany and Ireland provided about 70 percent of the immigrants arriving here between 1820 and 1840. The "push" factors of overpopulation and economic dislocation in Europe combined with the "pull" of a country that had a farm for any family willing and able to clear and work it. As towns and commerce developed, there were also jobs digging canals, building railroads, unloading ships and working in manufacturing. A constant flow of immigrants was needed to fill these and a thousand other positions because, in this free and growing nation, any hod-carrier could take his family west and claim his own home-stead.

The flow of immigrants continued to increase: between 1841 and 1860, 4,311,465 arrived. More than 87 percent were from Ireland, Germany and Great Britain. Some Prot-estant Americans were concerned by the sudden influx of so many Catholic Irish and Germans, fearing the impact of large numbers of people with different languages and religions. But the problems of black slavery and the sectional rivalries that culminated in the War Between the States overshadowed those differences. A more serious problem than those of language and religious differences was created in 1854 when the Gold Rush in California led to the importation of Chinese coolies. American working men saw the poorly-paid Chinese laborers as a threat to their very existence.

State legislatures reacted to the sudden influx of Chinese laborers by enacting laws aimed at excluding them. Then, in 1875, the U.S. Supreme Court ruled that state laws regulat-ing immigration unconstitutionally restrained interstate com-merce. That year, after a century in which the federal govern-ment left immigration largely unregulated, public demand led Congress to pass legislation to restrict the entry of Chi-nese coolies. When Chinese immigration continued despite the law, Congress passed another measure, popularly known as the Chinese Exclusion Act, which significantly reduced Oriental immigration. The thirty years of substantial Chinese immigration before 1882 had seen about 220,000 Chinese come to our shores. By that year, the total population of the United States had grown to more than 50 million.

As the 1880s began, the immigrant flow seemed to many native Americans to have become a torrent. The Supreme Court's 1875 ruling had thrown out all state immigration laws, many of which had long excluded convicts, lunatics, idiots and other persons likely to become public charges. So the first general immigration restriction statute enacted by Congress in 1882 excluded those persons and imposed a 50¢ per person tax on immigrants. Other restrictive immigration laws followed during the 1880s and 1890s, with the aim of reducing the entry of the Chinese and contract labor which depressed American wages.

Despite federal legislation, the decade 1881-1890 saw 5,246,613 immigrants arrive, more than twice the number during any previous ten-year period. The frontier was coming to an end, yet the rapid growth of American industry demanded a plentiful supply of cheap labor. Steamship companies, eager for cross-Atlantic fares, sent agents to scour the nations of Europe, telling credulous peasants of fortunes, or at least high wages, to be made in America. Matching the flow of immigrants with the needs of the economy became a problem — and it is one which has reappeared today. Big business, as a general rule, favored large-scale immigration because the large pool of laborers kept wages down. Working men naturally feared being reduced to the low wage scales of immigrants recently arrived from Palermo, Cracow or Peking.

In the 1880s the source of immigrants began changing from Northwest Europe to countries in Southern and Eastern Europe, such as Russia, Italy, Poland, and Austria-Hungary, as the table on the following page demonstrates.

Many Americans were alarmed by the "new immigrants." Northwest Europe had been the source of about 95

European Sources of Immigration to the United States 1820-1910

Decade	Northern & Western Europe (%)	Southern & Eastern Europe (%)
1820-1830	68.0	2.2
1831-1840	81.7	1.0
1841-1850	93.0	.3
1851-1860	93.6	.8
1861-1870	87.8	1.5
1871-1880	74.6	7.2
1881-1890	72.0	18.3
1891-1900	44.6	51.9
1901-1910	21.7	70.8

percent of the immigration to the U.S. from the founding of the first colonies until 1883. The new immigrants grouped together in ethnic enclaves and seemed intent on retaining their foreign languages, religions, and cultures. Some followed alien political doctrines such as socialism and anarchism. They congregated in the large cities -- often existing in abject poverty. Most native Americans still lived in rural areas and distrusted what Thomas Jefferson once referred to as the "rabble" of the cities. The new immigrants frequently became the pawns of corrupt political machines. Their strangeness, combined with their sheer numbers, alarmed many of the descendants of the "old immigrants," who had conquered the wilderness and built the nation over more than two centuries. Public demand led to new restrictive laws in the 1890s and in the first decade of the twentieth century, including expansion of the excluded classes to include paupers, epileptics, beggars, persons with contagious diseases, anarchists, prostitutes and procurers, and also provided for an increase in the head tax to $4.00.

While the flow slowed somewhat in the decade 1891-

1900, the U.S. was soon faced with the greatest flood of immigrants in the nation's history, chiefly from Southern and Eastern Europe. In addition, Japanese immigrants began entering on the West Coast, where their low standard of living and high birth rate seemed to threaten to drive white Americans from California. By treaties, this influx was slowed, but public pressure for a total ban continued, leading to the Immigration Act of 1917, which again increased the excluded classes, and for the first time imposed a requirement of basic literacy in some langauge.

After the First World War, the dislocations in Europe threatened to send even greater numbers of immigrants to a United States which was itself suffering from unemployment and a housing shortage. Public pressure mounted for a new approach that would finally reduce the *number* of immigrants. All of the previous laws imposing qualitative tests had failed to reduce the numbers of immigrants to a level acceptable to the American people.

In 1921, a stop-gap quota law was passed to limit the number of foreigners entering to three percent of foreign-born people of that nationality living in the U.S. in 1910. There were numerous exceptions, but the net effect was to limit immigration to about 358,000 per year.

The Immigration Act of 1924 phased out the temporary 1921 law, replacing it with a national origins plan to take effect in 1929. The national origins system set an annual quota (originally 153,714) to be apportioned among the countries to which it applied. Each country was able to send immigrants in proportion to that nation's past contribution to the population of the United States. This Act and the 1921 Act significantly reduced immigration from Southern and Eastern Europe. The 1924 Act can be seen as an attempt to maintain the ethnic status quo. President Calvin Coolidge expressed the prevailing sentiment in his message to Congress on December 6, 1923, when he said:

American institutions rest solely on good citizenship. They were created by people who had a background of self-government. New arrivals should be limited to our capacity to absorb them into the ranks of good citizenship. America must be kept American. For this purpose it is necessary to continue a policy of restricted immigration. It would be well to make such immigration of a selective nature with some inspection at the source, and based either on a prior census or upon the record of naturalization. Either method would insure the admission of those with the largest capacity and best intention of becoming citizens . . . . Those who do not want to be partakers of the American spirit ought not to settle in America.

Because many more people from Southern and Eastern Europe wanted to enter the U.S. than were permitted by the new national origins plan, and because the quotas given Northern European nations were larger, cries of "discrimination" began. These complaints did not end until the national origins feature was eliminated from our immigration laws in 1965.

The Great Depression was the major factor in drastically reducing immigration in the 1930s, when it dropped below even the levels allowed by the 1924 Act.

After World War II, immigration increased rapidly due to a series of enactments to bring in refugees, displaced persons, foreign war brides and others over and above the quotas. Although the Immigration and Nationality Act of 1952 retained the national origins system, an increased number of nonquota immigrants, such as immediate relatives of U.S. citizens, were allowed. As in the past, there was no limit placed on immigrants from the Western Hemisphere.

An essential purpose of the national origins quota system retained by the 1952 Act was to limit the total number of admissions to our shores. Yet, with the active support of President Eisenhower, who had opposed the 1952 law as too restrictive, Congress continued to pass special legislation admitting large numbers of refugees. Between 1945 and

1960, the U.S. admitted over a million refugees and spent more than $1 billion in their behalf.

Cuban refugees began entering the country in large numbers with the fall of the Batista regime in 1959. By the end of the 1970s, we had 700,000 Cubans in America, chiefly in Florida, New York and New Jersey. Our role as leader of the free world, along with our traditional humanitarian concerns for refugees, led our leaders to be very generous. The American economy was growing rapidly. Unemployment was low.

The trend toward liberalizing our immigration laws culminated in the Immigration and Nationality Act Amendments of 1965, which abandoned the national origins idea and any vestiges of racial discrimination for a system based primarily on reunification of families and skills needed in the U.S.

Eastern Hemisphere immigration was limited to 170,000 annually, with a 20,000 maximum per nation. In order to treat all nations equally, and to limit increasing immigration from Latin America, the 1965 statute imposed for the first time an annual ceiling of 120,000 on Western Hemisphere immigration, effective in 1968. Not surprisingly, given his political support from Hispanics, Senator Edward Kennedy opposed putting any limit on Latin American immigration.

The new law increased the total number of immigrants and shifted most new immigration from Europe to Latin America and Asia. Elimination of the longstanding stringent limits on Asian immigration has led to a flood of immigrants from countries like India. The table on the following page compares immigration for 1956-65, the last decade under the old law, to 1967-76 immigration.

Note that immigrants from India went from 5,416 in 1956-65 to 115,800 in 1967-76, an increase of 2,038 percent. European immigration fell 27.4 percent, while total Asian immigration increased 369.2 percent. Despite official limitations on immigration from Latin America and the Caribbean, overpopulation, poverty and proximity to the U.S. have encouraged increasing migration from those nations. The

Immigration by Country of Birth
Fiscal Years 1956-1965 and 1967-1976
(Selected Countries)

Country of Origin	1956-1965	1967-1976	Percent Change
Total	**2,878,153**	**3,883,153**	**+34.9**
Europe	**1,400,051**	**1,016,110**	**−27.4**
Germany	309,762	89,211	−71.2
Greece	46,494	129,076	+176.4
Italy	197,261	200,279	+1.5
Portugal	28,977	122,306	+322.1
Sweden	20,850	8,262	−60.4
United Kingdom	248,650	147,135	−40.8
Asia	**224,342**	**1,052,688**	**+369.2**
China and Taiwan	43,455	166,480	+283.2
Hong Kong	5,965	45,608	+664.6
India	5,416	115,800	+2,038.1
Iran	5,161	21,984	+326.0
Korea	16,361	166,422	+917.2
Philippines	27,621	270,078	+877.8
Africa	**22,924**	**63,978**	**+179.1**
Egypt	6,986	25,966	+271.7
Nigeria	677	4,787	+607.1
Uganda	82	2,283	+2,684.1
Oceania	**11,916**	**30,207**	**+153.5**
North America	**1,050,983**	**1,507,434**	**+43.4**
Canada	321,682	138,945	−56.8
Mexico	419,770	550,964	+368.1
Cuba	132,267	302,638	+128.8
Dominican Republic	40,047	121,818	+204.2
Haiti	13,154	56,387	+328.7
Jamaica	14,853	130,404	+778.0
Trinidad & Tobago	3,646	59,728	+1,538.2
South America	**167,772**	**212,778**	**+26.8**
Argentina	32,269	25,699	−27.1
Colombia	46,955	60,665	+29.2
Ecuador	22,620	43,361	+91.7
Guyana	2,135	23,029	+978.6
Uruguay	2,023	6,159	+204.4

Source: U.S. Interagency Task Force on Immigration Policy, Staff Report, March 1979.

quotas are filled, but the overflow comes anyway, illegally.

The new law was passed overwhelmingly, amid self-congratulations on our generosity. When it was enacted, unemployment was under five percent, inflation was only four-and-a-half percent, and gasoline cost 30¢ a gallon. We thought we could police the world and take in its castoffs. Our leaders were not able to see even as far as the next decade.

An increasingly crowded and strife-torn world continued to produce refugees and immigrants in growing numbers. More than 560,000 Indochinese entered the United States between the fall of Vietnam and Cambodia in 1975 and the end of 1981, and a steady flow continues. The Refugee Act of 1980 defines "refugee" as a person who is "unwilling or unable to return to his country . . . because of persecution or a well-founded fear of persecution on account of race, religion, nationality, membership in a particular social group or political opinion." This definition is ignored in practice. One study of Vietnamese "refugees" found that only eight percent were genuine refugees; most left for economic reasons or to avoid military service. In addition, the law authorizes federal assistance for the resettlement of refugees, which has cost more than a billion dollars annually in recent years. As the 1980s began, with twelve million Americans out of work, shortages of resources, and the federal government over a trillion dollars in debt, foreigners continued to pour in from every corner of the earth.

In 375 years we have civilized and populated a virtually empty continent. Fifty million immigrants, from English Pilgrims to Vietnamese boat people, multiplied to produce a population of more than 226 million people by 1980. For over a century we have had laws placing limits on immigration. Today we no longer have the work force requirements of an underpopulated nation with a rapidly expanding economy. Now we must set immigration limits to meet modern conditions of massive unemployment, resource shortages and overcrowding.

But our immigration laws are not working as they should. In 1980 more foreigners came to our land than in any previous year in our history. What is wrong with our immigration laws? The next chapter takes a look.

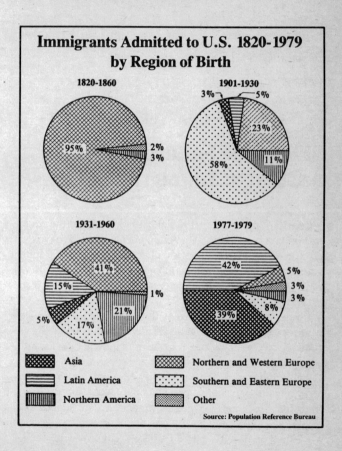

Immigrants Admitted to U.S. 1820-1979 by Region of Birth

1820-1860

95%
2%
3%

1901-1930

3%
5%
23%
58%
11%

1931-1960

41%
15%
21%
1%
5%
17%

1977-1979

42%
5%
3%
3%
8%
39%

Asia

Northern and Western Europe

Latin America

Southern and Eastern Europe

Northern America

Other

Source: Population Reference Bureau

CHAPTER 2

The Failure of Our Current Immigration Laws

Legislation passed in 1976 and 1980 modified the Immigration and Nationality Act Amendments of 1965 to create a system with an overall worldwide ceiling of 270,000 quota immigrants per year, with a maximum of 20,000 immigrants per country. The preference categories are detailed on the next page.

Immigrants become citizens through naturalization. This requires five years continuous residence in the United States, good moral character, belief in the principles of our Constitution, and the ability to read, write and speak simple English.

The Immigration and Nationality Act contains 33 grounds for exclusion of aliens. For example, would-be third and sixth (occupational) preference immigrants are supposed to be allowed entry only if they will not depress the wages and working conditions of U.S. workers employed in similar occupations.

Other types of aliens who are supposed to be excluded are the insane, sexual deviates, drug addicts, criminals, prostitutes, and persons likely to go on welfare. There are 19

The Current Preference System

Pref-erence	Visa numbers allocated up to:	Immigrants included:
1	20% of 270,000	Unmarried adult sons and daughters of citizens, naturalized and native-born, and their children
2	26% of 270,000	Spouses, unmarried sons and daughters of permanent resident aliens, and their children, plus unused in category 1
3	10% of 270,000	Persons of exceptional ability in the arts, sciences and professions, and their spouses and children
4	10% of 270,000	Married sons and daughters of citizens and their spouses and children, plus unused in categories 1 and 2
5	24% of 270,000	Brothers and sisters of citizens, naturalized and native-born, and their spouses and children, plus unused in categories 1, 2 and 4
6	10% of 270,000	Skilled or unskilled workers in short supply, their spouses and children

Note that only 10% of the legal entry slots are set aside for workers (and their families) whose talents are actually needed in the United States (sixth category entrants).

grounds for deportation under current law, many of which are similar to the reasons for excluding would-be entrants. However, the laws dealing with the exclusion and deportation of aliens are not strictly enforced, due to pro-alien court rulings by liberal federal judges and severe manpower shortages in the Immigration and Naturalization Service (many INS visa inspectors have to review over 100 applications *per hour*). Liberal judges have ruled that aliens can go on welfare as soon as they arrive here, despite the law (8 U.S. Code, section 1251(a)(5)) which expressly requires the deportation of aliens who ''within five years after entry become a public charge . . . ."

The ceiling of 270,000 legal immigrants is deceptive, since large numbers of immigrants are "exempt from numerical restrictions." Those people legally permitted to enter, but not counted against the "ceiling" of 270,000 per year, include the following:

Outside Current Preference System

Immediate relatives of citizens	Unrestricted
Special immigrants (small number usually associated with international agencies)	Unrestricted
Refugees, theoretically limited to 50,000 per year by the Refugee Act of 1980	Unrestricted, in ad hoc fashion
Doctors, investors and other small groups	Unrestricted

To show how this works in practice, in the year 1982, an estimated total of 617,000 immigrant visas were issued. The following major groups came to the United States above the preference ceiling of 270,000:

Immediate relatives	155,392
Adjustment of refugees and family members	173,000
Special immigrants	(est.) 3,000
Asylees	2,000
Fiances	5,700
Doctors and investors	3,400

Failure to count "immediate relatives" of United States citizens aged 21 and over against the annual ceiling of 270,000 legal immigrants has allowed thousands of additional aliens to enter our country every year. For example, in 1979 the number of persons entering under this category was 149,000 and passed 155,000 in 1982. Justification for permitting this generous loophole, as its major congressional defender, Peter W. Rodino, has argued, is that the primary objective of our immigration laws since 1965 has been "family reunification," regardless of the impact on the U.S. job market or the possibility that these people may become dependent on welfare programs. Defenders of liberal immigration contend that it is cruel to separate families. In most cases the United States citizen in question is a foreigner who comes to this country, becomes a naturalized citizen, and then sends for the rest of his family. In a comment entitled "Immigration: Who Is Family?" even the editors of the liberal *Washington Post* (September 13, 1982) observed:

> In the category of brothers and sisters (the "fifth preference"), a backlog of more than 700,000 people is waiting for visas. The group is large because it includes, of course, all the spouses and minor children of the siblings who have an automatic right to come along. In one case, a single (naturalized) citizen petitioned for all her brothers and sisters, their spouses and their children: 69 people . . . .
>
> It would be nice if grandparents and cousins and aunts and nephews could all come together to America as families did a hundred years ago. But with a fixed number of places available priorities have to be assigned.

This is one of the major loopholes permitting countries like India, Korea, Mexico and the Philippines to exceed the 20,000 per country limit year after year. When most Americans think about reuniting a "family," they tend to refer to the immediate family consisting of parents and children who usually reside together. The tie between parents and children and between a husband and wife living together supersedes the link between the husband and his relatives and the wife and her relatives. However, as immigration expert Dr. Arthur Corwin explains, "In Third World cultures there is a strongly felt obligation to bring in members of the extended family, with or without visas, so that the number of dependents grows."

Critics of the present permissive immigration system, including many immigration officials, have pointedly asked: Why should brothers and sisters in distant lands be awarded special visa preferences merely because one of the family decided to move to the United States, and then decided to become a U.S. citizen? Or, became a U.S. citizen merely because he happened to be born on U.S. soil? Even if we assume that family reunification should be achieved by permitting relatives of United States citizens to enter, there is still no good reason why immediate relatives should not be charged against the annual quota of 270,000 legal immigrants.

As a veteran Capitol Hill insider recently observed, "a more realistic explanation for the exemption of immediate relatives and refugees from any numerical limitation is that it allows politicians to tell concerned citizens that we have a 270,000 annual limit on immigration, when, in fact, real numbers admitted are much larger." The chart on the following page shows just what he means.

The other major group of aliens currently exempt from the 270,000 per year quota are "refugees." Refugees are often permitted to enter or allowed to stay here by special legislation. Furthermore, the Immigration and Nationality Act has long given the U.S. Attorney General "parole" authority to allow aliens to enter our country for reasons deemed "strictly in the public interest." This authority was used to bring in vast numbers of Hungarian, Cuban and Indochinese refugees.

The inconsistent nature of previous federal responses to refugees prompted Congress to pass the Refugee Act of 1980. This law defines a refugee as a person who cannot return to his country because of fear of persecution on account of race, religion, nationality, social group or political opinion. This internationally accepted definition requires that the person claiming to be a refugee have a legitimate fear of persecution. A person trying to leave a country and enter the United States because of economic conditions, or be-

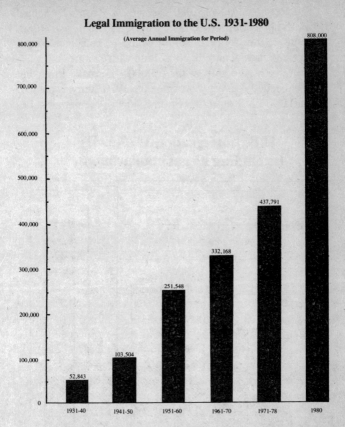

Legal Immigration to the U.S. 1931-1980

(Average Annual Immigration for Period)

cause his country does not have a representative form of government, is not a refugee. This makes sense, given the fact that most people on earth live in nations with a lower standard of living than is presently enjoyed in the United States, and that all but a few countries are governed by authoritarian regimes. If we disregard a strict interpretation of what constitutes a "refugee," the U.S. may have to accept more than *three billion* people who might like to come here as "refugees."

The Refugee Act of 1980 assumed a "normal" annual flow of up to 50,000 refugees through fiscal year 1982. Thereafter, the "normal" flow would be established each year by the President after consulting with Congress.

We have yet to stop at the 50,000 "normal" limit, but have exceeded it every year since the 1980 Act was passed. The 50,000 limit on refugee admissions is meaningless be-

U.S. Immigration 1976-1981
(excluding illegal immigration)

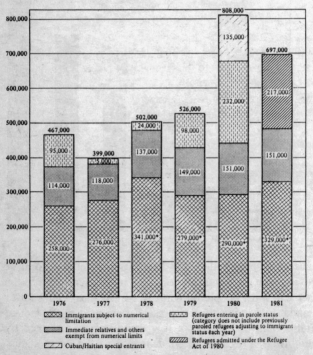

Immigrants subject to numerical limitation

Immediate relatives and others exempt from numerical limits

Cuban/Haitian special entrants

Refugees entering in parole status (category does not include previously paroled refugees adjusting to immigrant status each year)

Refugees admitted under the Refugee Act of 1980

* Includes part of the 145,000 extra numerically limited visas as a result of the Silva v. Levi court decision.

Source: Select Commission on Immigration and Refugee Policy

cause the law permits the President to allow in even larger numbers after consultation with Congress when an "emergency" exists and "grave national concerns" require larger admissions. This is a loophole large enough to enable tens of thousands of additional aliens to enter our country every year. Under existing federal law, refugees can obtain permanent resident status after living here a year. The law also provides taxpayer-funded public assistance to refugees for up to three years after entry.

The Refugee Act of 1980 was given its first test just a few weeks after it passed. As we will see in the next chapter, Congress and President Carter flunked the test miserably.

CHAPTER 3

Refugees -- and "Refugees"

In the spring of 1980, the Carter Administration welcomed thousands of illegal aliens who poured into South Florida. As the boatloads of Cubans from Mariel Harbor arrived in the United States, it soon became clear that most of these people were not genuine refugees. They were not fleeing persecution because of their political or religious views, their social class or their race. It turned out that many were common criminals, loafers, homosexuals and average non-political citizens who had heard of or even seen the prosperity of the Cubans already living in the United States. In the late 1970s Castro allowed some Cuban Americans to visit Cuba. Said Enrique Torres, a Havana auto mechanic: "Seeing all those watches and good clothing -- it blew people's minds."

Jack Watson, Jimmy Carter's Assistant for Intergovernmental Affairs, explained the decision to accept the illegal Cubans in April 1980: "We decided that it would be counterproductive to enforce the laws." The Carter Administration did not want to offend the politically powerful Cuban-American voting bloc, which now holds the balance of power in

Florida politics. Congress had just passed the 1980 Refugee Act defining refugees and limiting the overuse of the Attorney General's parole authority by providing that only 5,000 persons granted asylum could be given permanent resettlement status annually. Yet the parole authority was used to allow more than 125,000 Cubans to remain in the United States, whether they were actual refugees or not. As asylum applicants, these aliens immediately began to receive federal "benefits" (including food stamps), despite the fact that Congress was supposed to be fighting mounting budget deficits. Congress then passed legislation, signed into law by President Carter on October 10, 1980, giving Cuban and Haitian "entrants" almost all of the generous welfare benefits genuine refugees receive. In addition, Congress authorized special adult education programs for these uninvited immigrants from the Caribbean. The politicians failed to see the irony in creating such programs for foreigners illegally entering our country at a time when educational programs for American veterans had been reduced.

As if Florida did not have enough problems from the thousands of Cubans, recent years have seen a constant flow of Haitians into that beleaguered state. In 1980, 15,093 Haitians were caught trying to enter the United States illegally. The November 30, 1981, issue of *U.S. News & World Report* revealed that "from 300,000 to 400,000 Haitians now are living in America, most of them illegal entrants." Poverty lawyers (financed by the liberal National Council of Churches), Roman Catholic charities and the taxpayer-funded U.S. Legal Services Corporation began representing these illegal Haitians. They flooded the courts with claims that the Haitians were political refugees entitled to full asylum hearings -- and numerous appeals. Thousands of Haitians had to be housed in federal detention centers, while others were released on their own recognizance -- and immediately disappeared into the burgeoning Haitian colony in Florida. INS, State Department and Justice Department officials investigating the influx found that the "refugees" were fleeing

Haiti's poverty, and were not genuine political refugees. Art Brill, a Justice Department spokesman, said that "they are illegal aliens." Despite those findings, black civil rights leaders in this country began claiming discrimination because illegal Cubans had been permitted to stay here in 1980, while half-hearted attempts were made to exclude some of the illegal Haitians. By the end of 1980, the U.S. Attorney General simply paroled many of the Haitians who arrived in this country.

Both the Carter and Reagan administrations have proposed legislation to let the paroled Haitians and Cubans stay permanently. In late 1984, the Reagan administration began giving legal permanent resident status to many of the "Marielito" Cubans, with no complaint from Congress. The Haitians are still held at the Krome detention center near Miami, and have shown their displeasure with the slowness of the process by periodically rioting. Like the Cubans, the Haitians have added to Florida's staggering welfare bill and are costing taxpayers hundreds of millions of dollars every year, with no end in sight.

In the face of mounting public outrage, the Reagan Administration has acted to cut the flow of illegal Haitian entrants from a floodtide to a modest stream. From the thousands of Haitians who came in during the last months of the Carter Administration, the number was cut to 333 for the year 1983. The Reagan Administration ordered the Coast Guard to intercept boatloads of Haitians heading for our shores, detained others who arrived illegally, and refused asylum requests. These measures slowed the flood of Haitians and clearly show that when our government is determined to act, the flow of illegals can be sharply reduced.

Indochinese "refugees" have continued to pour into the United States, though it has been ten years since the fall of South Vietnam. According to the State Department, 73,522 arrived here in 1982, and 93,408 in 1983. (As one American veteran of the Vietnam War ruefully observed, "if all the 'refugees' had helped us fight the Communists, we would have won the war.") By the close of 1984, the U.S. had taken in more than 500,000 Indochinese.

The first wave included genuine refugees: people who had sided with the U.S. in the war and would have been persecuted by the Communists. But today, many refugees from Vietnam are ethnic Chinese merchants who buy their way out of that country in order to come to the United States. Others from Cambodia and Vietnam are young men trying to avoid service in the armed forces of their nations, according to the findings of the respected *Far Eastern Economic Review,* which concluded in 1981 that "the majority of those now leaving Indochina are not political refugees but economic migrants." Despite the weight of evidence, the State Department continues to insist that all Indochinese seeking to come to the U.S. be classified as refugees. Voice of America broadcasts encourage people in Indochina to flee in boats, and then the U.S. 7th Fleet picks them up at sea. While Asian nations -- including Japan -- turn away the boat people, the United States government seeks them out.

The liberal media have tried to convince the American people that the Indochinese fit right into the mainstream of American life. The reality is quite different.

The Chairman and Vice-Chairman of the San Diego County Board of Supervisors wrote to President Reagan on April 3, 1981, to inform him that the 24,000 Indochinese refugees who had arrived in their area up to that time were not being "integrated in the social and economic life of this country . . . . Dependency on public assistance in San Diego County among Indochinese refugees approximates 53%." A 1981 study by the National Association of Counties and the National Governors' Association found that 64.8 percent of Indochinese refugees in 11 states were receiving public cash assistance. More than 90 percent of the Indochinese refugees coming to San Diego and San Francisco apply for welfare benefits within weeks of their arrival. As of the beginning of 1984, welfare use by refugees was running close to the 70 percent figure.

The Indochinese are not melting into the American population. Instead, most are congregating in a few large cities. According to testimony given on behalf of the National Association of Counties to the Senate Judiciary Committee, two-thirds of all Indochinese refugees reside in only 40 of the nation's 3,104 counties. According to Joseph Diaz, a California state official, 200,000 Indochinese refugees have settled in California, but their numbers quickly swelled to about 250,000 because of new births. Asian families with ten children are not uncommon. Many are illiterate farmers who speak no English. In California there have been a number of ugly incidents of outraged Americans surrounding the homes of Indochinese thought to be killing and eating neighborhood pets. Cambodians and Laotians have been discovered catching and eating squirrels, ducks and dogs found in public parks. A bill to make it a crime to kill dogs or cats for food was voted down in 1981 after Asians in the state complained that such a law would be "discriminatory."

San Diego officials report growing conflicts between refugees and native Americans over jobs and housing. Economic competition has led to violence between American and Vietnamese fishermen in Texas, where an American was killed in 1979. Two Vietnamese were charged with the crime.

Disputes among blacks, Chicanos and Vietnamese living in public housing projects in Denver have also resulted in violence. Yang Chee, a spokesman for Laotians in Colorado, reported in 1983 that many new Laotian "refugees" think Colorado puts too many restrictions on welfare and other public aid and because of this many Indochinese are moving to California, where the programs are "totally different and much better."

The 125,000 Cuban "Marielitos," an unknown number of Haitians and the more than 560,000 people from Indochina are now being joined by "refugees" from Central America. Like Mexico, the countries of Central America have experienced a "baby boom" (which is still in progress) that dooms millions of people to a life of poverty. In addition, Communist-backed revolutionary movements are disrupting the fragile economies of such nations as El Salvador and Guatemala. Governments in this area which should be devoting their energies toward solving their population and related economic problems are instead forced to contend with leftist insurgency.

The impact of population pressure on political and economic conditions in Central America and other less developed countries is misunderstood by many people. General William Westmoreland, currently a trustee of the Population Crisis Committee, gave a good explanation of the problems created by overpopulation in El Salvador:

> In the last 30 years, El Salvador's population has grown from about 1.9 million to 4.8 million. In the same period, the urban population has almost tripled. While modest population increases might spur economic growth in some countries, it is ludicrous to argue that population growth of this magnitude and rapidity in a country with fragile political institutions, a poor natural resource base and widespread poverty, can be anything but destabilizing.
>
> This issue is not zero population growth . . . . Even if Salvadoran families decided today to have no more than two children apiece, the country's population would still double. But it would double in 70 years instead of 27 years, for families in El Salvador are currently averaging over six children apiece. The issue is El Salvador's ability to cope. Slower population growth buys time to cope.
>
> El Salvador and most of its Central American neighbors are clearly not coping. For the region as a whole, unemployment and severe underemployment are conservatively estimated at 40 percent. With 65 percent of the population under age 25, further massive labor force expansion is inevitable. A third to a half of the mushrooming city populations are slum dwellers.
>
> Except in Costa Rica, population growth and urbanization have overwhelmed government and private investments in housing, sanitation, health care and education. Even in countries with strong governments and democratic traditions, the

growing concentration of unemployed youth in congested
slums close to the seats of power, represents a security threat
of substantial proportions, exploitable by extremists . . . .

Under these conditions, it is simply a matter of common
sense that U.S. efforts to bring political stability and economic progress to El Salvador must include efforts to moderate
population growth . . . .

The *Los Angeles Herald Examiner* of May 8, 1984, revealed that some 250,000 Salvadorans are currently living in
the Los Angeles area and that before long it is expected that
10 percent of the entire population of El Salvador will be
living in the state of California. The California legislature
fears that "The cost to the state may become larger than the
[U.S.] economic assistance now budgeted to El Salvador."
Harold Ezell, Western regional commissioner of the INS,
said, "Illegal aliens victimize taxpayers by fraudulently obtaining millions of dollars worth of benefits and by occupy-
ing jobs which should be available to U.S. citizens and
permanent residents. And the Salvadoran children are entitled to public education in an already financially squeezed
public school system. The Salvadorans are also bringing
communicable diseases from the Third World to the United
States."

Take the case of a typical El Salvadoran in the United
States. His name is Jose Amaya-Reyes. He is male, 26 years
old and lives with eleven other Salvadoran illegals in a
two-bedroom apartment in San Francisco. He has a wife and
seven children back in Intipuca, El Salvador. Should Jose be
granted amnesty, he plans to bring his entire family to the
United States.

Jose entered the U.S. in 1980, just after he heard that
President Carter was going to give amnesty to illegal aliens.

Almost as soon as he arrived, Jose went to work for a
construction company making $5.50 per hour as a laborer.
After working just a few weeks, Jose was able to obtain a
fraudulent Green Card and a valid Social Security number.

Jose was arrested by a local law enforcement officer after

the car that he was driving smashed into two parked cars. Jose was not injured. After being processed for drunken driving, Jose was turned over to the Immigration Service. He then admitted that he was here illegally.

During his interview with the INS, the following information was obtained:

• Jose sends $400 per month to his wife and brother in El Salvador.

• He pays Social Security, but claims *ten* dependents on his W-4 form, so almost no income tax is withheld (and Jose has never filed an income tax return).

• He has money saved to pay his drunken driving bond and he has the card from an immigration lawyer who told him to call if he was ever arrested by the INS.

• Jose knows nothing about the fighting going on in his country, except that the government troops are fighting the rebels.

• He has no particular political affiliation, and does not know whether the money he sends home is being used to buy food or guns -- or both.

After Jose calls his attorney, he is released on $500 bond and told to appear in three weeks for his deportation hearing. The following day, Jose's attorney files an application for political asylum in the United States. He is granted a permit to work while the application is pending.

As a political asylum applicant, Jose can now collect unemployment compensation because he lost his job (apparently for drinking). He is also eligible for welfare and food stamps. If the police begin looking for him, he can simply leave and go on to another apartment with a number of other Salvadoran illegals.

Jose is now collecting welfare from the state and federal governments, paying no taxes, and has been granted permission to stay and work if he wishes. But he cannot be located in case the government needs to contact him.

The news media portray all the "Joses" in our country as hard-working, scared refugees from oppression. In reality, most of these people are simply economic refugees who only serve to take jobs from American citizens and drain our Social Security, welfare and other benefit programs.

Not all of the "refugees" from Central America are simply looking for work or welfare. Others are leftist opponents of the anti-Communist governments of El Salvador and Guatemala. Since 1980, liberal Americans have been operating an "underground railroad," which has assisted untold numbers of such people into the United States. *U.S. News & World Report* of September 13, 1982, carried a story about "Smuggling Aliens into U.S. -- Booming Business," which included a report on "When Churches Turn Smugglers." The magazine drew attention to Rev. John Fife, minister of Tucson, Arizona's Southside United Presbyterian Church, whose congregation is in the forefront of efforts to bring illegal aliens from Central America to our country. The *Arizona Republic* of March 21, 1984, reported that the "underground railroad" operated by Rev. Fife was formed "to protest U.S. policy in Central America." The organization has spread into a network of about 110 churches in approximately 60 cities nationwide. Proponents of "liberation theology" and "Christian Marxism," active among almost all denominations, have been aiding this effort on both sides of the border. On May 15, 1984, a 29-year-old church worker, Stacey Lynn Merkt, was convicted in Brownsville, Texas, of conspiring to smuggle two illegal aliens from El Salvador into the U.S. She has long been active with other "religious" opponents of U.S. policy in Central America. It is noteworthy that these same American churchpeople have shown little or no sympathy for anti-Communist Nicaraguans trying to overthrow the Sandinista gang which seized power there in 1979, nor are they supportive of anti-guerrilla efforts in El Salvador and Guatemala. There is no question but that some of the Central Americans are taking advantage of U.S. churchgoers by claiming to be "political" refugees when, in fact, they are simply looking for a better economic future in this country. Others brought into the U.S. are leftists who may contribute to our own internal security problems.

The cost of these hundreds of thousands of "refugees" to U.S. taxpayers is staggering. The federal government has been spending billions of dollars on refugee-related programs in recent years. The State Department has specific multi-million-dollar annual programs for "refugee" transportation to the U.S., reception and placement grants and "English as a Second Language" courses. The Department of Agriculture's Food Stamp program provides additional millions of dollars of assistance to "refugees" every year. And the Department of Health and Human Services conducts a wide range of programs for the exclusive benefit of "refugees." These include education assistance for children of refugees, preventive health care services, Cuban and Haitian special programs, Aid to Families with Dependent Children, Medicaid and Supplemental Security Income (SSI). Astonishingly, the vast majority of HHS economic assistance going to "refugees" is administered and disbursed by the Social Security Administration. Indeed, the Office of Refugee Resettlement is an administrative component of Social Security.

The cost of "refugee aid" by the Departments of State, Agriculture, and Health and Human Services (including Social Security) amounted to $1,131,800,000 in 1981 and $1,082,500,000 in 1982. But this is only part of the cost to taxpayers.

Hundreds of millions of dollars more are spent by state and local governments for aid to "refugees" and illegals. Although Congress must accept responsibility for unwillingness to enforce our immigration laws, the federal government provides relatively little assistance to states which bear the brunt of the alien invasion.

As bad as the situation is now, the problem presented to the U.S. by "refugees" is bound to get much worse in the future if corrective measures are not quickly enacted and then strictly enforced. Freedom House, a respected non-profit organization which makes annual surveys of political rights and civil liberties in countries around the globe, reports that 111 countries and 27 related territories, with over 3 billion people, are "partly free" or "not free" at all. These countries are also among those with the highest rates of population growth. There is bound to be constant turmoil and dislocation as people and nations fight for survival. Millions upon millions of people will want to flee to the relative safety and prosperity of the United States.

But we cannot take in the whole world.

CHAPTER 4

The World
Population Explosion

We have to find a way to gain control of our borders . . . .
The economy within the United States can never keep up with
the fertility pressure outside of the United States.

Gov. Richard D. Lamm (D-Colo.)
"Face the Nation," CBS-TV
May 20, 1984

The "Population Explosion" is no longer a futuristic
concept belonging in a science fiction novel. It is taking place
before our very eyes. A Georgetown University study warns
that "Endemic poverty, historically unprecedented levels of
unemployment, and related political and social unrest are
emerging as major world forces, with massive international
migration a prominent result."

It took from man's first appearance on earth until about the
year 1850 for the world's population to reach one billion. The
total number of people in the world reached two billion in
1930. The three billion mark was reached in 1960; the fourth
billion was added by 1975. The world's population is now
estimated at more than 4.6 billion. World overpopulation is

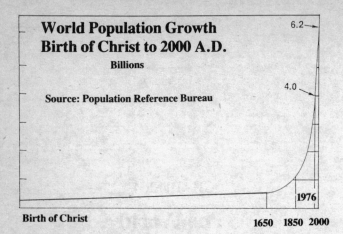

World Population Growth
Birth of Christ to 2000 A.D.

Billions

Source: Population Reference Bureau

6.2

4.0

1976

Birth of Christ

1650   1850 2000

real and steadily growing worse.

Beginning first in Northern and Western Europe, modern sanitation and medical practices drastically reduced the infant mortality rate and led to steady increases in the average lifespan. Lacking effective birth control practices, Europe's population grew rapidly as the high birth rate interacted with a falling death rate. Luckily, these surplus people were able to migrate to sparsely settled areas of North and South America and Australia, where more people were needed and welcomed. Between 1840 and 1930, over 50 million people left Europe for other parts of the globe. Today, with modern birth control and in light of the detrimental impact of the two world wars of the first half of this century, the population of most European nations is growing very slowly, or even declining, thus practically ending the pressure to emigrate.

The source of today's world population explosion is found among the underdeveloped nations of Africa, Asia and Latin America. Europeans and Americans have introduced modern medicines and sanitation practices to these areas. Modern discoveries in the field of antibiotics and disease control programs have brought down infant mortality. Nutrition has also been improved, with such countries as the United States,

Canada and Australia growing large surpluses of grains and other foodstuffs. Many people survive today who yesterday would certainly have starved or succumbed to some fatal illness. The result has been a steady fall in the death rate.

Unfortunately, most people in Third World nations have not yet begun practicing birth control. The contrast between Western and Third World birth rates is dramatically shown in the following table.

High Birth Rate Nations (selected examples)		Low Birth Rate Nations (selected examples)	
Vietnam	41	East Germany	14
Nigeria	50	West Germany	9
Niger	51	Sweden	11
Kenya	51	Britain	12
Philippines	41	United States	15.4
Mexico	42	Canada	15
Haiti	43	Italy	13
Dominican Republic	42	France	14
India	34	Norway	13

(figures are live births per 1,000 population)

The high birth rates in less developed countries are particularly alarming when we realize that such high birth rates exist in nations with populations much larger than the European states of the past. In 1975, 71 percent of the world's population lived in underdeveloped countries, and by the year 2000, an estimated 78 percent of earth's population will live in the Third World. By 2110 A.D., only 13 percent of the world's people will live in what are today's industrialized nations. More than 90 percent of the world population growth over the next 20 years will occur in the less developed countries.

The United Nations Fund for Population Activities estimated in 1981 that world population will level off at 10½ billion by the year 2110 A.D. Remember that there are "only" 4.6 billion people today. Where will another six billion people go? How will they be fed, clothed and sheltered? No one knows. United Nations expert Dr. T.N. Krishnan could only remark that these facts raised "problems about how we share our global resources."

Life in the poor nations of the world will grow even more miserable as this century comes to a close. Overcrowding, shortages of food and water, lack of jobs, political turmoil and other problems resulting from overpopulation will lead *hundreds of millions* to think of coming to America. A Kettering Foundation poll taken in the early 1970s found that one-third of the people in Latin America wanted to leave their native lands and 90 percent of those who wanted to emigrate wished to come to the United States. The population of Latin America in the year 2000 (less than 15 years away) will be 595 million, according to the Population Reference Bureau. Unless we learn to say no, we had better get ready to meet a lot of new neighbors.

Mexico's population is increasing at a phenomenal rate, with families of 7 or 8 children common. In 1960, Mexico had 34 million people, and by 1980 the population had more than doubled to 72 million. By the year 2000, Mexico's population is expected to mushroom to 129 million. The pattern is similar in Central America, where the population is doubling every generation.

In the past, the surplus rural populations of Mexico and Central America could find some work in their cities. This is no longer the case. The rural populations are already so large that there is not enough arable land to provide even a bare subsistence living for additional people. Many of the cities in this region are already badly overcrowded. Unemployment and underemployment (work for less than half the year) is running at a rate of at least 50 percent in Mexico, and is near that figure throughout Central America, where Communist insurgency is exacerbating already desperate economic conditions. Even if the Communists are defeated in El Salvador and Guatemala, and the Sandinista regime overthrown in Nicaragua, the economies of these countries will remain weak, due in large measure to the high levels of population growth. These conditions will inevitably lead millions and more millions of Mexicans and Central Americans to try to enter the United States.

Most Americans really have little notion of just what the combination of grinding poverty and overpopulation means. Alan L. Otten, writing in the *Wall Street Journal* of February 17, 1984, provides an insight into this situation:

> They are Central America's looming nightmare -- the constantly swelling ranks of teenage males who can't find work and who, unless an unexpected economic miracle occurs, won't find it any time soon. Even if the area's current military conflicts are resolved, the teens' accumulating numbers add up to a monster problem certain to trouble governments of right, left or center . . . .
>
> In addition to their potential for local explosion, these unemployed teenagers and young men raise another specter for the U.S. Illegal migration to the U.S. is an obvious escape valve for them; and there is ample evidence that just such a movement is under way, adding to (and often mingling with) the far larger flood of illegal Mexican immigrants.
>
> U.S. and Guatemalan officials agree that increasing numbers of Guatemalans -- as well as Salvadorans and Nicaraguans who have made their way to Guatemala -- are undoubtedly moving across the nations' borders into Mexico and thence, via some sort of Mexican underground railroad, on into the U.S. Local papers daily carry a score of advertisements inquiring "Do you want to travel to the U.S. without problem?" and promising "Trip 99% guaranteed." . . .
>
> Central America's population has almost doubled in the past 23 years, from 11.2 million in 1960 to 21.9 million in 1983. Assuming only a modest drop in fertility rates over the next 15 years -- by far the likeliest assumption -- the numbers will increase sharply again, to 37 million, by the year 2000 . . . .

As The Environmental Fund has pointed out, "The U.S. has been accustomed to influencing Central America without being much influenced by it. Suddenly, we are deeply affected by events over which we have little control."

Until very recently, Central America has not been a major source of immigrants to the United States. Less than 100,000 immigrants arrived in the U.S. from Central America during the decade of the 1960s, and approximately 111,400 arrived here in 1971-1979. Illegal immigration from that area has been rising steadily. In a single district of Los Angeles, an estimated 200,000-plus Salvadorans are residing. Nicaraguans, Guatemalans and others are joining the flood of Mexicans in a great migration to the United States. And corrupt politicians and religious leaders in Mexico and Central America are only too glad to siphon off their excess population, rather than come to grips with problems that are of their own making.

In Africa, the continent with the highest population growth rate in history, the impact of overpopulation is already being felt. Food production per person fell 14 percent during the 1970s. Some of this shortfall is made up by food imported (often donated) from the United States, Canada, Australia and other advanced countries. But population growth in the developing countries is so rapid that we are beginning to witness agricultural production falling hopelessly behind the production of people. Pressure is mounting for these people to either starve or try to flee to the "land of plenty" -- the United States.

Desperate inhabitants of Third World countries such as India are depleting natural resources at a frightening rate. These poor people customarily heat and cook with wood. As population increases, trees are being cut down faster than they can be replaced with saplings.

Can these gloomy consequences of overpopulation, misery and starvation be prevented by a reduction of the birth rate of Third World countries? Sad to say, the reduction in birth rates needed to avoid disaster would have to be far greater and faster than anything likely to take place. High fertility rates in recent decades have produced very youthful populations in the Third World. Even if the average number of births per woman drops dramatically, the number of women of childbearing age will continue to grow for decades, leading to a continuing rapid increase in population. The relative youth of the populations of the Third World is illustrated by the fact that 23 percent of the population of Canada, the United States and Europe is under the age of 15, while 40 percent of the population of Latin America is under that age.

In earlier eras of world history, one solution to overpopulation was migration. But today there are no empty continents. With millions of our own citizens out of work, with shortages of oil, electricity and even water, the United States certainly does not need more people. Despite our problems, the United States still looks like a land of plenty to the masses of the Third World. So they try to enter by the millions.

Can the United States solve the world overpopulation problem by taking in much of the excess population of the Third World? Some sentimental liberals say we should try. But the population of the Third World will grow by at least two billion over the next 25 years. Can the United States -- a nation of 235 million -- take in this many people? Of course not. But if we permit the alien flood to pour in for many more years, we will witness the destruction of the peaceful and prosperous country our ancestors built and bequeathed to us.

CHAPTER 5

Immigration
and the U.S. Population

Many Americans, after reading stories about the low
U.S. birth rate, might conclude that our population must not
be growing very fast -- that we may have reached a condition
of Zero Population Growth (ZPG). In fact, the reverse is true.
Today, the United States has the fastest rate of population
increase of any developed country in the world. The cause of
this increase is immigration, legal and illegal.

The current birth rate is 1.9 births per woman, perhaps the
lowest in our history. However, because there are so many
"baby boom" young women of child-bearing age, our population would continue to grow gradually for another 50 years
even without any immigration. Without immigration, the
U.S. population would peak at 268 million by the year 2030
A.D. (up from 226 million in 1980). Overcrowding, pollu-
tion and shortages of oil and other resources might continue
to be major problems due to the pressure exerted by these
additional 42 million people, but we would have 50 years to
adjust and attempt to come up with rational solutions.

What will the situation be if large-scale immigration continues? In 1980, 808,000 legal immigrants were permitted to enter the U.S. Since then, legal immigration has continued to number over 600,000 per year. Estimates of net annual illegal immigration range from several hundred thousand to over two million. Using two different assumptions, we can come up with rough estimates of total annual immigration to the U.S.: a low, very conservative figure of one million immigrants (counting both legal and illegal) per year, and a more realistic assumption of two million every year. Should Congress enact some form of mild employer sanctions and give a modest increase in resources to the now overburdened Border Patrol, it would be possible to reduce -- but not stop -- the flow of illegal aliens, thus reducing overall immigration to the one million a year figure. The following table shows the U.S. population increase resulting from both assumptions.

Effect of Immigration on Future U.S. Population

Year	Annual Net Immigration 1,000,000		Annual Net Immigration 2,000,000	
	Total Population	Additional Population Compared to No Immigration	Total Population	Additional Population Compared to No Immigration
2000	267,127,000	23,450,000	290,578,000	46,901,000
2030	310,371,000	65,536,000	375,907,000	131,072,000
2050	320,935,000	93,620,000	414,555,000	187,240,000

(Note: Assumes 1.8 births per woman.)

What would the U.S. be like with over 400 million people? Even with approximately half that number, the U.S. has been paying a heavy price. During the past decade we have suffered from oil and other energy shortages, the loss of farmlands and forests, lowered water quality and spot water shortages, smog and acid rain. The Department of Agriculture reports that some three million acres of land are being taken annually to build roads, homes and other urban projects. In 60 of the 106 water resource subregions of the United States, groundwater resources are being used faster than they are recharging. All of these strains on our environment will intensify if the U.S. population continues to expand.

The following table illustrates how many new mineral resources are required annually for each person in the United

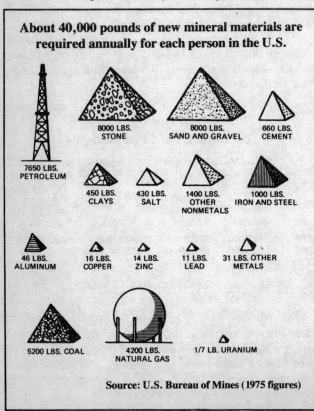

About 40,000 pounds of new mineral materials are required annually for each person in the U.S.

7650 LBS. PETROLEUM

8000 LBS. STONE

8000 LBS. SAND AND GRAVEL

660 LBS. CEMENT

450 LBS. CLAYS

430 LBS. SALT

1400 LBS. OTHER NONMETALS

1000 LBS. IRON AND STEEL

46 LBS. ALUMINUM

16 LBS. COPPER

14 LBS. ZINC

11 LBS. LEAD

31 LBS. OTHER METALS

5200 LBS. COAL

4200 LBS. NATURAL GAS

1/7 LB. URANIUM

Source: U.S. Bureau of Mines (1975 figures)

States. Considering how much material is needed to sustain our current population of approximately 234 million, imagine what would be required to meet the needs of a population much larger because of virtually unrestricted immigration.

Think of the burden that will be placed on all of our resources by the extra 187 million people we will have by 2050 A.D. if immigration continues at two million per year. A number of American cities are already unbearable as places of habitation. Further overcrowding and ethnic strife will make urban conditions that much worse. Domestic resources such as water, natural gas and timber will be rapidly depleted (as is already the case in several overpopulated Third World countries). Our already dangerous dependence on foreign nations for oil and dozens of strategic minerals will grow dramatically.

Assuming that immigration is not brought under control, what kind of people will inhabit the overcrowded United States of the future? This problem has been studied by Dr. Leon F. Bouvier, one of America's leading population experts. According to Dr. Bouvier, ''because of the decline in [American] fertility and continued net immigration, immigrants and their descendants will become an even greater portion of the total U.S. population in future years.''

Based on the experience of the past decade, the size and origin of the current world population growth, and our present immigration laws, most of these future immigrants to the United States will be from the Caribbean, Latin America (people of generally mixed Indian-Caucasian and Negro-Caucasian racial backgrounds), Asia (for example, Chinese, Koreans, Indochinese, Indians and Pakistanis) and the Pacific Islands (for example, Filipinos). Dr. Bouvier estimates that 45 percent of our future immigrants (both legal and illegal) will be Caribbean/Latin American, 40 percent Asian and Pacific Island, and 15 percent from other countries, such as Canada and the nations of Europe and Africa. To keep his projections from becoming too complex, Dr. Bouvier assumes that new immigrants will have the same fertility rate as Americans once they settle here. He admits that this "may result in an *under-estimate* of the impact of immigration on the U.S. population" because of a high immigrant birth rate.

The results of Dr. Bouvier's studies are cause for concern to every responsible American citizen. If immigration continues at the rate of one million per year, by 2050 A.D. (within the normal lifespan of a child born today), 29.2 percent of the U.S. population will be made up of post-1980 immigrants and their descendants. If annual net immigration remains at two million per year, by 2050 post-1980 immigrants and their descendants will constitute 45.2 percent of our population, and by the year 2080, they will account for more than half -- 56.9 percent.

The changing ethnic composition of America is revealed by the 1980 Census, which found 14,605,883 Hispanics (people of Mexican, Puerto Rican, Cuban and other Latin American background) constituting 6.4 percent of our total population. This represents a 61 percent increase from the 1970 Census, which found 9,072,602 Hispanics.

By comparison, the American black population showed an increase of 18 percent over the same ten-year period, and the Asian population grew by a staggering 122 percent! During that ten-year period, the white population rose a mere 6.47 percent (approximately one-tenth that of Hispanics, one-third that of blacks, and one-fiftieth that of Asians). When you add the existing minority populations to the post-1980 immigrants and their descendants, and then consider the very high birth rates of Hispanics and blacks, it becomes clear that the white majority will become the minority sometime during the coming century -- unless immigration is greatly reduced.

The import of an immigration policy that permits the ethnic composition of this country to shift so decisively should be obvious. But as Professor Garrett Hardin of the University of California writes in his book, *Naked Emperors: Essays of a Taboo-Stalker* (Los Altos, Calif: William Kaufmann, Inc.), "We become a passel of poltroons who quail at the word 'minority.' We have lost our common sense." And Professor Georges Fauriol points out in his important study, *U.S. Immigration Policy and the National Interest* (Center for Strategic and International Studies, Georgetown University, Washington, D.C.):

> The long run implications of our current "head in the sand" attitude about maintaining de-facto open borders are indeed serious. They go to the heart of our security as a nation, our domestic political unity, our economic prosperity, and our role in the international system. Illegal immigration is by its very nature causing pressures beyond those associated with heavy immigration flows in particular and population growth in general.
>
> Opposition to "open borders" or support for immigration reform has for too long been erroneously characterized as representative of a return to "nativism," of an emerging racism. This has led to an unwillingness to examine the more serious and important aspects of U.S. immigration policy.

As dramatic as the change in the ethnic composition of our nation seems, the effect on several large states will be even more pronounced. The Population Reference Bureau points out in its publication, *U.S. Population: Where We Are; Where We're Going,* that over 70 percent of the new immigrants reside in six states: California, New York, Texas, Florida, Illinois and New Jersey. Immigrants usually go where others from their homeland have settled. Most Cubans are in Florida; most Mexicans go to Texas, California and Illinois; Filipinos and Koreans favor California. According to the Immigration and Naturalization Service, 31.5 percent of Asian immigrants and 28.4 percent of Latin Americans will settle in California. If annual immigration is just one million and present patterns of residence continue, almost 21 percent of California's population will be post-1980 immigrants and their descendants by the year 2000 -- only 15 years from now. By 2030 A.D., 42.3 percent of California's population will be made up of post-1980 immigrants. At the one million a year rate, New York State will be 19 percent post-1980 immigrants by 2000. At an annual immigration rate of two million, by the year 2030, California, New York, Illinois, Florida and Texas will have majorities composed of post-1980 immigrants and their descendants.

A hint of the political impact of this change was seen during the 1984 Presidential balloting. While President Reagan received approximately 60 percent of the total popular vote, the opposite was the case among the groups which form over 80 percent of current immigration to America. Orientals preferred liberal Democrat Walter Mondale by 54 to 46 percent and black voters supported Mondale by a 91 to 9 percent margin. Hispanic voters likewise gave most of their votes to Mondale, who received 72 percent of the Hispanic vote in the state of Texas. These figures raise the question of whether it will be possible to elect a conservative presidential candidate in the future, should massive Third-World immigration continue.

It should be kept in mind that, for the sake of simplicity, all of the population projections discussed have assumed that new immigrants will have the same birth rates as American citizens do at present. It is more realistic to assume that the immigrants will, at least initially, keep the large families that are characteristic of their homelands and only gradually approach the lower, balanced birth rates prevalent among our majority population. According to the National Center for Health Statistics, the Mexican-American fertility rate is 119.3 births per 1,000 women, over 90 percent higher than the rate for non-Hispanic women (see table).

In sworn testimony before a Senate committee in 1981, Harvey Rubin, Dade County (Florida) Commissioner, reported that "one out of every four babies born in the county hospital is born to a Cuban/Haitian entrant" (referring to the 1980 and 1981 "refugees").

The high Hispanic birth rate and level of immigration is dramatically shown in the changing composition of Cali-

Birthrates and Fertility Rates, by Hispanic Origin: Nine States, 1979

Ethnic group	Births per 1,000 population	Births per 1,000 women aged 15-44
All origins	15.6	66.7
Non-Hispanic	14.7	63.2
All Hispanic	25.5	100.5
Mexican American	29.6	119.3
Puerto Rican	22.6	80.7
Cuban	8.6	39.7
Other Hispanic	25.7	95.9

Note: The nine states are Arizona, California, Colorado, Florida, Illinois, Indiana, New Jersey, New York and Ohio.

fornia's schools. Guillermo Lopez, chief of the California Department of Education's Office of Bilingual-Bicultural Education, says that "the first sign of the tide to come" are figures showing that "Anglos" (English-speaking whites) comprised 65 percent of the 12th grade enrollment in the Los Angeles Unified School District, but only 12 percent of the 1982 kindergarten classes. Ramiro Reyes, Associate State Superintendent of Public Instruction in the California Department of Education, cites statistics highlighting the dramatic demographic shifts in California:

• Minorities now make up 48 percent of the total school enrollment, but were only 25 percent in 1967.

• Between 1967 and 1979, the number of Hispanic students increased by 51 percent.

The numbers are inexorable. There is no escaping this basic fact: an advanced Western country with a balanced birth rate that lets in one or two million Third World immigrants every year will eventually have a Third World majority. As the growing population surpasses our resources, living conditions will worsen and the United States will become more and more like the poverty-stricken countries the recent wave of immigrants are fleeing.

One of the great liberal propaganda feats of the 20th century has been to convince many Americans that massive immigration is an essential part of the American way of life. But as Lindsay Grant and John H. Tanton wrote,

> As a nation, we have obligations to our own people and to the future of our land which should be balanced against the general urge to help others. No country, not even the United States, can absorb the present population explosion. It can only be met in each country where it is under way. To offer haven to the few who escape is to forget the many who cannot, and an expanding American population does not necessarily advance the common good . . . . (From "Immigration and the American Conscience," 1981).

During an economic boom, more people may be needed; at a time of recession and unemployment, no additions to the population are called for. This fact is too often clouded by emotional references to the Statue of Liberty.

The Statue of Liberty was erected on an island in New York Harbor in 1886. It had absolutely nothing to do with immigration, as is evident from the words on the dedication plaque: "A gift from the people of the Republic of France to the people of the United States. This statue of Liberty Enlightening the World commemorates the alliance of the two nations in achieving the independence of the U.S., and attests their abiding friendship." Only later, in 1903, was the poem welcoming tired, poor, "wretched refuse" inscribed on a plaque on the statue's pedestal. As millions of immigrants sailed past the statue, they came to associate it with immigration and their new lives in the United States. Today, as millions of immigrants pour in from nations where liberty and free government are largely unknown, we may come to see our liberty crushed by the immigration floodtide -- bringing an ironic end to the life of the Lady in the Harbor.

CHAPTER 6

Our Relations
with the Third World

The exploding population and endemic poverty of the Third World is leading hundreds of millions of people to consider emigrating to the United States. The root cause of our immigration crisis is that our political leaders have failed to enforce existing laws and to pass reforms needed to deal with the rising alien flood. With determined leadership, supported by an informed public, the U.S. can stop illegal immigration and reduce legal immigration to levels which best serve the future interests of the American people. But the question remains: Is there anything we can do to help the poor of the Third World?

The world's population is expanding at such a rate that even if the U.S. admitted 500 million foreigners over the next 25 years, we would only be taking in a quarter of the additional population of the poor countries. And were we to do this, it would destroy our nation, its culture and economy -- and even then, this would not alleviate the harsh conditions in the Third World.

Massive foreign aid is not the solution. As *U.S. News &*

World Report has noted, ''Despite more than 150 billion dollars in foreign aid poured into these [Third World] countries by the United States alone since World War II, hunger and poverty are more of a global condition today than twenty years ago.'' In a review of Western aid to poor countries, British economists P.T. Bauer and B.S. Yamey explained that ''such transfers weaken the West . . . . And they do not promote economic improvement . . . . Foreign aid has more often than not helped to bring to the fore governments hostile to the market system and sympathetic to the Soviet bloc . . . . Official transfers cannot significantly promote development . . . . Transfers enable governments to pursue policies which patently retard growth and increase poverty. Such policies include restrictions of the economic activities of productive minorities; controls on the inflow of foreign capital, enterprise and skills; restraints on the activities of traders and the destruction of distribution networks; and price policies which discourage the production of food and other farm products.''

U.S. immigration policies are hurting less developed countries. We currently admit thousands of highly trained people, such as doctors, nurses and engineers from such places as India, Pakistan and Jamaica -- countries where their skills are desperately needed. Pakistan alone loses 50 percent of its medical school graduates every year. How will these countries ever control their populations and develop their economies if badly needed, well-educated personnel continue to leave?

Sad to say, few Third World governments place a high priority on family planning and genuine economic development. Most of them will spend some money on population control, particularly when it is given to them by Western nations. But they prefer to devote their own resources to armies and advanced weapons, grandiose government buildings and public works projects, and estates and luxury cars for the top officials.

An objective observer, looking at the exploding populations and terrible poverty of countries such as India, Ethiopia and Mexico, may assume that their governments would concentrate on solving their internal problems. Instead, we find India spending millions of dollars on a space satellite and on developing nuclear weapons. In addition, the people of India have failed to develop attitudes and conduct conducive to economic progress. Insect pests, such as cockroaches, are protected on religious grounds, and sacred cattle compete with humans for food, instead of contributing to the food supply.

Political and cultural factors account for starvation in Africa, and loud demands are being made of Western nations to pour billions of dollars in aid into that continent. Professor Harding Le Riche of the University of Toronto, author of *Overpopulation and Third World Immigration*, has responded to the guilt-mongering that characterizes much of the media's coverage of the Ethiopian famine.

> Is not the government of Ethiopia responsible for its own people? This communist state can apparently afford to maintain a 300,000 strong army, trained and equipped by the Russians. And what do the Ethiopians do with their army? They oppress their own people and those around them . . . . Some of us have known for years that there is going to be massive starvation in Africa. There are many reasons for this. One is that African governments, in general, have not been interested in stimulating agriculture to feed their own people. Some of the ruling elites love cash crops, so that they can put the cash in Swiss banks. Then there is the enormous population growth in Africa since 1930 when the population was about 140 million. Now it is about 400 million and in some countries populations are doubling every 17 years. Many, if not most African leaders refuse to recognize that their populations are growing too fast; that there are limits to growth.

Because of its long common border with the United States, illegal immigration from Mexico is the greatest immigration problem we face. As former CIA Director William Colby said in 1978, ''The most obvious threat to the United States is that there are 60 million Mexicans and there are going to be 120 million of them by the end of the century.'' Although rich in oil and other resources, Mexico's economy is in a shambles and government corruption flourishes. From 1947 until the early 1970s, *faster* population growth was official policy in Mexico. Today, the Mexican family planning program gets only one one-thousandth of the government budget. Yet the total amount of pesos (the equivalent of billions of dollars) raked off by PEMEX oil directors and even the chief of police in Mexico City during the recent administration of Lopez Portillo could have funded the most effective family planning program in the world, with money left over to teach each peasant more effective farming techniques. Far from enacting needed economic reforms, the current Mexican government is actually extending stifling economic controls. According to an article in *Time* for August 6, 1984, ''Ten years ago, government officials [in Mexico] managed about 25% of the economy; today they manage about 75%, ranging from oil production to supermarkets and parking lots.''

Speaking before the Senate Armed Services Committee in 1984, General Paul Gorman, chief of the U.S. Southern Command until March 1, 1985, characterized Mexico as ''the most corrupt government and society in Central America'' and warned that it is likely to be our ''Number One security problem'' within the next ten years. He pointed out that the Mexican government ''has pursued a policy of accommodation with its own left and international leftist interests,'' and that Mexico City is becoming ''the center for subversion throughout Central America.'' In recent months reports have leaked out of Mexico about demonstrations and severe riots along the U.S.-Mexican border. *U.S. News & World Report* (Oct. 8, 1984) carried an article, ''Mexico -- Next Domino for Latin American Unrest?'' which stated that ''widespread poverty and a flood of refugees [from war-torn Central America] make the country's southern states ripe for a peasant uprising.''

It is argued by some in this country that the U.S. should take in Mexico's surplus population. Aside from the fact that we do not need more poorly educated people with few skills, our permissive immigration policies act as a ''safety valve'' for dissatisfied Mexican citizens who might otherwise demand substantive changes in the Mexican government, economy and society. Indeed, successive Mexican governments have deliberately encouraged many of its citizens to flee northward rather than enact needed political and economic reforms. And until the U.S. government closes our southern border to illegal immigrants, the Mexican government will feel little compulsion to end the pervasive corruption. As columnist Joan Beck wrote in the *Colorado Springs Gazette Telegraph* (July 28, 1984),

> Mexico has one of the highest birthrates in the world. Poverty and unemployment are pandemic. We cannot solve Mexico's problems by letting millions of people skip across our borders to add to our pools of poverty and dilute the resources with which we are trying to help our poor. Nor should we yield to the pressures of a growing, aggrieved and unassimilable minority to become a bilingual, bicultural society.
>
> It is wrong to argue that we must have illegal aliens to do our dirty jobs. Supporters of slavery made that argument . . . . The creation of another big group of exploitable workers who will be demanding affirmative action and entitlements is too high a price to pay for finding someone to pick the lettuce and clean up motel rooms.
>
> This nation, like every other, has a right to control its borders and define its population. No other country accepts such large numbers of legal immigrants or tolerates illegal immigration.

The United States is currently feeding millions of people around the globe. This year we will sell and give millions of bushels of grain to less developed nations. Our productivity and generosity keep millions from starving to death. Instead of gratitude, we receive insults and demands for even more assistance. A horrible truth has begin to dawn among clear-headed men and women in the West: our past generosity has allowed the populations of the Third World to expand to levels that cannot be sustained. Western food, medicine and sanitation practices have led to the population explosion rocking politically and economically primitive Third World countries. Winston Churchill was reported to have said of such places, ''We feed, they breed.''

Our aid has allowed Third World populations to expand to the size where their leaders think they can threaten us with their sheer numbers. A leading spokesman for this element, Algerian President Houri Boumedienne, charged in 1974, ''[N]o quantity of atomic bombs could stem the tide of billions of human beings who someday will leave the poor southern part of the world to erupt into the relatively accessible spaces of the rich northern hemisphere looking for survival.'' That spectre is unfolding in the United States today, not because we cannot stop the alien invasion, but solely because our politicians have not even tried to stop it.

Many people in the West are unaware that the extreme poverty found in so much of the world is essentially self-inflicted. After studying problems of economic development in the Third World, British Economist P.T. Bauer came to the conclusion that

> Income and living standards in the West are the outcome of many centuries of cultural and economic progress; they have not come about in one or two generations. It is therefore not surprising, abnormal or reprehensible that many Third World countries (notably in Africa) which do not have centuries of progress behind them should have much lower incomes than the twentieth-century West. . . . The West began poor and progressed without external aid . . . . Moreover, Western societies progressed in conditions far more difficult than those facing the Third World, which can draw on huge external markets, on external capital markets, on a vast range of technology and on diverse skills unavailable before. Plain-

ly, official aid is not indispensable for progress . . . . In so far as development prospects of many Third World countries are unfavorable, this has nothing to do with external factors. Economic achievement depends on people's attributes, attitudes, motivations, mores and political arrangements. In many countries the prevailing personal, social and political determinants are uncongenial to material progress: witness the preference for a contemplative life, opposition to paid work by women and widespread torpor and fatalism in certain countries. *(Equality, the Third World and Economic Delusion,* Harvard University Press, 1981).

We can help the Third World by providing emergency assistance to those nations that prove -- not just promise -- they are serious about ending corruption, building viable, free economies and limiting population growth. If they do not want such ''strings'' attached to our help, they are free to pursue the sort of policies which have led to the critical conditions found in so many countries. If that sounds cruel, we must realize that additional aid to irresponsible governments will allow populations to continue to balloon, leading hundreds of millions to die of starvation and disease in decades to come, rather than the millions who are suffering today. The sooner Third World nations have to face reality and begin taking care of their own people, the better off they -- and we -- will be.

CHAPTER 7

Illegal Immigration

"There are today in the United States six to eight million illegal aliens, and that number is increasing by half a million to a million each year," said General Leonard Chapman, Commissioner of the United States Immigration and Naturalization Service (INS) in 1976. Every observer of the problem agrees that the flow of illegals has steadily increased since General Chapman tried to warn the public nine years ago. General Chapman, commandant of the U.S. Marine Corps before President Ford appointed him head of the INS, pleaded with Congress for two years to give his agency the manpower and legislation necessary to stop this alien invasion. Congress refused to help.

In 1977, President Jimmy Carter removed General Chapman as head of the INS. He appointed Leonel J. Castillo, a Mexican-American politician from Texas, whose philosophy of law enforcement was summed up in an interview with *U.S. News & World Report* when he said of illegal immigration, "I don't think you can stop it."

Castillo worked to make this prophecy self-fulfilling by personally taping "public service" radio broadcasts telling illegal aliens that they had constitutional rights, by preventing INS investigators from looking for illegal aliens in workplaces and residences, and by generally showing his sympathy for illegal aliens. Castillo attempted to downplay the gravity of the problem by asserting that there were "only" three to six million illegals here and by ordering INS officials to label illegal aliens as "undocumented workers."

Castillo's views have not been shared by members of the administration that replaced Jimmy Carter. In 1981, Attorney General William French Smith told the Senate Subcommittee on Immigration and Refugee Policy that the United States has "lost control of its borders." Smith told the Cabinet that illegals are now coming in at the rate of one-and-a-half to two million every year.

How do aliens enter this country illegally? Most illegal aliens sneak across the border, often at night, evading the U.S. Border Patrol (an arm of the INS). Others use fraudulent documents to get in, posing as U.S. citizens, legal resident aliens or foreigners with valid entry visas. The INS estimates that as many as 500,000 illegals enter the United States every year using false documents. Hundreds of thousands of other aliens fly into the United States with legitimate tourist or student visas and then disappear into the country and refuse to leave, often finding haven in the ethnic enclaves of our large cities. Such actions are, of course, in violation of U.S. laws.

Thousands of aliens arrange fraudulent marriages to American citizens so they can remain here. Professional "matchmakers" have been caught by federal agents arranging such marriages for Haitians, Liberians, Nigerians, Pakistanis, Mexicans and other foreigners. Crooked lawyers and others in this racket often receive fees of $1,400 to over $4,000 to set up the fraudulent marriages to Americans, who receive $500 to $600. Some Americans have had hundreds of fraudulent marriages to foreigners, who gain permanent resident status once they are married to a U.S. citizen, even if a divorce quickly follows.

Due to the vast numbers of illegal aliens apprehended every year -- more than 1.2 million -- it is rare for an alien to be put in jail or even formally deported. Instead, those from Mexico (who constitute the vast majority of all aliens apprehended) are simply driven or flown back to the Mexican border by the INS and released on the other side of the line. They often sneak back into the United States that same day or night. Some have been apprehended as many as *five times* in a single night, and when such a determined lawbreaker is not caught a sixth time, it would seem that he has at last been successful.

Where do they come from? Based on apprehensions and several studies, the leading source country is Mexico. Because our Border Patrol forces are concentrated on the 2000-mile-long Mexican border, 90% of those apprehended are Mexicans. But experts estimate that only 60% of the illegals come from Mexico. Large numbers of illegal aliens also come from Colombia, El Salvador, Canada, Guatemala, the Dominican Republic, Jamaica, Ecuador, the Philippines, South Korea, India, Thailand, Peru, Greece, Nigeria, Haiti and elsewhere. Most are Spanish-speaking people from Latin America. Almost every source country is poor and suffering from rapid population growth. Many of the illegals entering from Canada are actually from Asian or Latin American countries who know that our northern border is even less well guarded than our border with Mexico.

How do the illegals get here? Mexicans can simply walk across the border or wade across the Rio Grande and melt into the large Mexican-American neighborhoods of U.S. cities located near the border. In many cases, professional smugglers take trucks full of illegals as far north as Chicago. Salvadorans and others from Latin America also come through Mexico.

Others, such as Haitians, use the services of professional alien smugglers. Such smugglers in Haiti, for a fee of $500 or more, will buy the meager possessions of a Haitian (perhaps a small plot of land) and help him get a plane ticket to Montreal, Canada, posing as a tourist. The flight lasts only about four hours. Upon arrival in Canada, the smuggler loads a van full of illegals and drives to a point near the American border, where he lets the aliens out to walk through the woods and around the Border Patrol port of entry. The smuggler then drives across the border legally in his empty truck and picks up the illegals down the road. Five hours later he deposits them in Boston or some other U.S. city far from the border.

It is so easy to get people into our country this way that alien smugglers are known to offer a money-back guarantee, according to Gordon Dilmore, deputy chief patrol agent.

Every year millions of foreign tourists, businessmen and students enter the U.S. The terms of their visas require them to leave within a certain time limit and forbid them to take jobs here. According to a study prepared by Professor Daniel R. Vining, Jr., covering the years 1969 to 1978, as many as 500,000 aliens entered by commercial airlines, overstayed their visas and disappeared into our general population each year. This figure has grown to the point where today 700,000 more people enter the United States through our airports than leave. Many of these illegal aliens, commonly called "visa abusers," are well-educated and take good jobs here. They tend to congregate in ethnic enclaves of major metropolitan areas.

Why can't the Border Patrol stop this invasion? Despite the fact that General Chapman warned Congress in 1975 that illegal immigration was a serious problem, Congress has refused to give the Border Patrol and its parent agency, the INS, the manpower and equipment to handle the growing flood of legal and illegal aliens. From 1971 to 1984, the number of Border Patrol officers on duty was only increased from 1,564 to 2,628. Over the twenty-year period 1963-1983, apprehensions of illegal aliens went up 3000 percent, but the INS staff has increased only 50 percent. There are more law enforcement officers working on Capitol Hill protecting Congress than there are Border Patrolmen guarding our southern border with Mexico. On a normal work shift, between 300 and 400 officers try to guard the entire 1,945-mile border -- an impossible task for such few patrolmen. Despite their small numbers, apprehensions have been rising. During 1983, the INS caught a record 1.25 million illegal aliens.

Aliens Apprehended
Fiscal Years 1964-1983

Year	Apprehensions
1964	86,597
1965	110,371
1966	138,520
1967	161,608
1968	212,057
1969	283,557
1970	345,353
1971	420,126
1972	505,949
1973	655,968
1974	788,145
1975	766,600
1976	875,915
1976TQ*	221,824
1977	1,042,215
1978	1,057,977
1979	1,076,418
1980	910,361
1981	975,780
1982	970,246
1983	1,251,357

* Adjustment quarter for change in end of fiscal year.

The increased number of apprehensions is not due to increased vigilance or manpower. Rather it is the result of the rising tide of mass migration from the poor nations of the world to the United States. The influx is so large that some of the aliens almost literally bump into the overwhelmed members of the Border Patrol.

The INS has stated for the record that they catch around one out of three illegals trying to get in. Privately, officers in some areas have admitted that they often catch only one illegal alien out of eight. The Border Patrol is so underfunded that, on some days, officers cannot patrol the border at all because they do not have enough gasoline for their vehicles.

How many illegal aliens are there in the United States already? Because illegals hide from authorities, the exact number can never be known. In mid-1975, a study commissioned by the INS estimated that there were around eight million illegal aliens in the U.S. A report entitled "Illegal Aliens: Invasion Out of Control," in *U.S. News & World Report* of January 29, 1979, said that "as many as 12 million illegals may be in the U.S. today." The Environmental Fund, an authoritative, non-partisan research organization that studies the impact of overpopulation, concluded that New York City and Los Angeles together have more than three million illegals.

Under President Carter, Leonel Castillo and the Census Bureau contended that the total number of illegal aliens was smaller, in the three to six million range. However, Castillo was trying to promote Carter's plan to give amnesty to illegals, and had every reason to cite a lower figure to keep from upsetting the public. The Census Bureau has been criticized for missing illegals in its 1980 count, and for undercounting the legal population of many areas.

There is an inconsistency between the official figures given for the total illegal alien population and the estimates of annual influx. Because the Border Patrol has electronic sensors in many sectors of the southern border, it is able to detect illegal crossings at night even when the manpower to capture the illegals is lacking. Combining this with interviews of illegals caught at the border, as well as those apprehended further inland, the Border Patrol can make a fair estimate of the number of illegals that it fails to capture. The conclusion is that at least three illegals get by for every one caught -- and this does not include the up to one million who fly into the United States each year and do not fly out. With border apprehensions passing a million a year, the number of illegal aliens getting into the United States annually may exceed three million, not the "official" figure of 500,000 to two million cited by some government officials and the leaders of pro-immigrant lobby groups.

The inconsistency in numbers is sometimes explained by the claim that many illegals eventually go home, although it is hard to see why they would leave the prosperity of the United States to return to the poverty of their native lands. Whatever the number of illegals here today, experts agree that the number is large and rapidly growing larger.

Where do the illegals go? In the past, most illegals worked in the fields in the Southwestern United States. Today, most go to the cities. Michael Piore of the Massachusetts Institute of Technology (MIT) says that "the recent growth of the alien population appears to be occurring in industrialized urban areas." *U.S. News & World Report* estimates that the great majority of illegal aliens are concentrated in the metropolitan areas of six populous states: California, New York, New Jersey, Illinois, Massachusetts and Texas. Once in our country, illegals spread across the nation. While many go to places like Los Angeles, San Antonio and El Paso, others go far inland where there are few INS agents. Hundreds of thousands of illegal Mexicans are already working in the Chicago area, a city with a high rate of unemployment for citizens.

How long do illegals stay in the United States? Numerous studies indicate that illegals from distant lands generally stay here permanently if they can. Years ago, Mexican illegals often returned to Mexico each year after earning money harvesting crops in the United States. Today that pattern has changed. Illegal Mexican aliens increasingly leave seasonal agricultural work for year-round employment in manufacturing and service jobs. The growing "Mexicanization" of areas of Texas, California, New Mexico and other states also makes it more attractive for illegals to stay in this country.

Why do illegal aliens come here? Because, compared with their native lands, the United States is rich. Most illegals can make ten times as much money, or more, in the U.S. than they can in their homelands, if they could find any job at all with populations increasing at incredible rates. As in most Latin American nations, Mexico's jobless receive no public assistance or unemployment compensation. The following table shows the contrast between the per capita income of the U.S. and several of the countries that export illegal aliens:

United States	$10,630
Mexico	1,800
El Salvador	639
Dominican Republic	1,221
Cuba	840
Colombia	1,112
Haiti	260
Philippines	779
India	150
Pakistan	280

The illegals come to the U.S. rather than to other developed nations because we are so close to the exploding poor populations of Latin America and also because we are the *only* developed country in the world that fails to control its borders. They come because American businesses are free to hire them. They come because it is relatively easy to sign up for welfare programs, even if they are not qualified to receive welfare. If illegals could get neither jobs nor welfare, they would not come here.

What kinds of jobs do illegals take? In 1981 Attorney General Smith told a Senate subcommitee that only 15 percent of illegal aliens work as agricultural laborers. Many illegals work in blue-collar industrial jobs, in construction and in service employment such as restaurants and hotels. Seven years ago, the INS reported that there were a million illegal aliens employed in light industry in this country. A raid by Labor Department officials in New York City exposed the shocking growth of garment industry sweatshops, employing illegal aliens, including children, where wages were as low as one dollar per hour. Yet many other illegals receive very good wages.

INS investigators in Chicago found illegals working in transportation jobs paying more than $10 per hour. INS Commissioner Chapman said in 1976 that "at least one million illegal aliens are holding good jobs that pay well . . . probably another two or three million are holding lesser paying jobs." Over the past eight years, these numbers have probably doubled or tripled.

The presence of millions of illegals in the labor market tends to drive down wages for lower-level jobs. Professor Robert Birrell concluded that the presence of millions of illegal aliens in the U.S. work force explained the fact that millions of working-class Americans earned wages so low that they were below the official poverty line, even when employed. Real wages for low-level jobs in the U.S. have been falling for years, due in large measure to competition from hordes of illegals accustomed to low foreign living standards. By contrast, in Australia, a country with a capitalist economy but which limits immigration to protect its citizens, poverty is primarily a problem of the sick, the aged and others unable to work.

Cheap alien labor also reduces the incentive to introduce new labor-saving machinery, thus retarding productivity. Businesses that use cheap illegal labor become dependent on it. As an illegal leaves for a better-paying job, a new illegal immigrant is needed, so there is a constant demand for illegal aliens.

These illegals cost the United States billions of dollars every year in food stamps, medical care, educational expenses, lost income taxes, unemployment payments to citizens thrown out of work by aliens, and other services. Cheap foreign labor is not cheap in the long run -- not for the wage-earning, tax-paying people of the United States.

CHAPTER 8

Documentation Fraud

A $1-million-a-year ring that provided counterfeit documents for illegal aliens and criminals was smashed by federal investigators who raided an upper West Side [New York] printing shop, authorities said yesterday.

Raiders said they seized bogus printing plates for Social Security cards; Puerto Rican birth certificates; baptismal certificates; auto insurance cards; Vermont auto ownership cards; city marshal certificates; voter registration cards and diplomas from Brandeis High School and Queens College.

So reported the *New York Times* of May 13, 1983. Lawrence Paretta, a district director of investigation for the INS, was quoted in the same article as saying, "52% of immigrants from the Dominican Republic use phony ID cards to gain entry into the U.S. Once here many of them use these counterfeit identities to get on welfare rolls."

Unfortunately, this is not an isolated case. As the article noted, "Federal officials said there is *no way* to determine how many phony documents are in circulation." Two years ago, Newton van Duren, an admitted forger of federal documents sold to illegal aliens, told members of the Senate Committee on Governmental Affairs that "If 2 percent was my part of it and over a number of years I produced 100,000 documents, obviously the market is something like 5 million.''

News stories regularly appear giving further evidence of the growing problem of identification fraud:

ILLEGAL ALIENS LINKED TO CHECK SCAM;
$2.5 MILLION STOLEN IN PAST 18 MONTHS

''The stolen checks were taken from mail boxes and either sold at a discount or *cashed with the use of counterfeit alien registration cards,''* officials said. (emphasis added)

Los Angeles Herald Examiner
Feb. 29, 1984

On September 9, 1983, the *New York Times* reported that a ''Flood of Bogus ID Papers Imperils Plan to Curb Aliens,'' while the *Los Angeles Times* of January 13, 1983, carried a story about ''60,000 Phony Immigration Cards Seized at L.A. Bus Depot.'' And the *Tampa Tribune* of May 14, 1984, ran a story about ''Illegal Cuban Immigrants Using Phony Passports,'' which revealed that ''More and more Cuban refugees are immigrating illegally into Florida from Central America . . . trying to enter the country with fake passports purchased in Panama and Costa Rica . . . . The majority come from Panama, where thousands of Cubans -- most of them close relatives of Mariel refugees -- wait to travel to the United States. The rest come from Costa Rica, where another large Cuban colony awaits U.S. visas.'' One of the illegal Cuban entrants said, ''In Panama, when people know that you are a Cuban, they offer to sell you a passport. It's very easy to buy a passport.'' The article went on to describe the ''underground'' smuggling operation that helps thousands of aliens to illegally enter the U.S.: ''Most smugglers are believed to operate out of Panama, where they arrange for Cubans to leave the country several ways -- directly to Miami with fake passports, to Mexico and then across the Mexican-

U.S. border or via the Bahamas.''

How has this problem originated? Unlike many other countries in the world, the United States does not have a specific national identity document or card which establishes the identity of the bearer to federal, state or local authorities. There have been several attempts to introduce legislation to this end, particularly with respect to issuing a more secure Social Security card. But these attempts have been repeatedly thwarted by cries that such an action would be a step toward the totalitarian regime described in the novel *1984*. Thus, at present, the identity of any individual, be he or she a citizen, resident alien or illegal alien, is established through a multitude of easily forged documents, including birth or baptismal certificates, Social Security cards and numbers, passports and visas, drivers licenses and, in the case of resident and non-resident aliens, various documents issued by the Immigration and Naturalization Service and the U.S. Department of State.

How can the millions of illegal aliens already in our country remain virtually immune from the INS, support themselves through employment and welfare (including food stamps and Aid to Families with Dependent Children) and even collect Social Security benefits? How can aliens who have been caught and deported by the INS after violating either the terms of their visas, entering illegally, or committing fraud against governmental agencies, return to this country and perpetrate the same crimes again?

The answer to these questions involves a problem which is now recognized as a collateral area in the field of immigration control -- the counterfeiting of identification forms and documents. The Senate Committee on Governmental Affairs, through its Subcommittee on Investigations, has studied this problem and the revelations were astounding:

First, the forgery of documents such as the common Social Security card ''is a major societal problem and is growing.''

Second, the cost to the American taxpayer is staggering in terms of benefits paid out and loss of federal tax dollars used to conduct investigations.

Third, there is little or no cooperation between various agencies issuing a variety of federal identification documents.

Fourth, little is done to prevent deported aliens from re-entering the United States using bogus documents, and

Fifth, most of the federal identification documents are either easily obtained through illegitimate means or are easily counterfeited, thus making federal documentation fraud one of the largest "cottage industries" in the United States and in certain countries that are the point of origin for many illegal aliens.

What are these abused documents and how are they obtained by illegal aliens? The documents most abused fall into the purview of three federal agencies: the Department of State, the Immigration and Naturalization Service and the Social Security Administration.

From the State Department, a foreign national who wishes to visit the United States, conduct business here, study in our schools or become employed while applying for U.S. citizenship, must obtain a visa, which is stamped into the foreign national's passport. Although there are several types of visas, non-immigrant (tourist and student) visas are the most prevalent, and to date there is no limit imposed by our State Department on the numbers of these issued. To obtain one, a foreign national merely presents himself to the U.S. Consular Office in his native country and is screened. The issuing office decides whether or not the applicant intends to leave the U.S. at the end of his or her stay. The total time available for the overseas screening interview is three minutes, sometimes even less. Moreover, little effort is made to investigate the identity documents presented by the visa applicant, and even when fraud is uncovered, through the use of false documents or misrepresentations of fact, the individual is often able to receive the desired visa anyway. The visa is the foreigner's entry ticket to our land of plenty and while most foreign visitors to the U.S. abide by the terms of their visas, and obtain them legally, those desiring to enter our country and remain here as illegal resident aliens have easy access by violating their visa restrictions, often using forged identification papers to obtain one in the first place, or even by counterfeiting the visa itself.

The second source of documents misused by illegal aliens is the Immigration and Naturalization Service. In addition to its responsibility for patrolling the borders of our country, the INS is charged with the processing of millions of foreign visitors once they reach our shores. To help do this, the INS uses a variety of forms. The most widely used is the I-94 "Record of Non-Immigrant Arrival and Departure." This form is filled out by the arriving foreigner in duplicate, noting the name, citizenship, passport number and status of the visitor, with a copy kept by the alien and the original filed with the INS. This document is so widely used and so lacking in security that commercial airlines often print their own versions. However, as the Senate Governmental Affairs Committee points out, "the only purpose of the I-94 is to serve as a record of entry or departure, not to record identity or entry eligibility." But, as this study further notes, "Unfortunately, INS has failed to realize that other agencies such as the Department of Agriculture and state Departments of Motor Vehicles rely upon the document to prove an applicant's identity and entitlement to food stamps or a driver's license." The document can be stamped "eligible for employment" or "refugee," thus giving the bearer entitlement to a multitude of government programs. What is more, the ink used for these special stamps is easily duplicated. According to regulations, the I-94 is to be surrendered to INS officials when the foreign visitor departs the country. But because of manpower shortages and a nightmarish record-keeping system, it is often years (if ever) before the INS is able to reconcile the arrival copy of the I-94 with the departure copy of the same form. Thus, as Colorado Governor Richard Lamm pointed out on "Face the Nation" (May 20, 1984), "700,000 more people fly into America than fly out.'' Where are they? The INS rarely knows!

Another frequently abused document issued by the INS is the I-20, a certificate of admission to study at American schools. A foreign national wishing to study at an American institution of higher learning will apply to the school and when accepted receive the INS Form I-20, either from the school or from its authorized representative in the area. The ''student'' then takes the I-20 to the nearest U.S. Consular Office and receives a ''student visa'' allowing him to remain in the U.S. as long as he remains a student in good standing. The I-20 is issued by the school directly and not by the INS and State Department officials, who have little or no time to check the credentials of the student or school in question. This practice thus gives schools a virtual *carte blanche* to admit foreigners to the United States for almost unlimited or unspecified lengths of time. As Pulitzer Prize winning author John Crewdson remarks in his 1984 book, *The Tarnished Door: The New Immigrants and the Transformation of America:*

> However well intentioned the efforts to open wide the doors of American schools and colleges to young men and women from other countries, such programs also have contributed heavily to illegal immigration. There are now more than 300,000 foreigners living in the United States on student visas, a figure that is expected to double in the next seven years. By 1990, unless restrictions are imposed, one U.S. college student in 10 will probably be a foreigner . . . . A good many of them do come here for an education, but many others come with no intention of studying or they stay on after graduating or dropping out of school. A recent spot check in Los Angeles showed that more than a quarter of the foreigners holding student visas there were not enrolled at the schools they were supposed to be attending . . . .

One would expect that students from the Third World would choose areas of study that would most benefit their home countries, such as health care, agriculture and other fields in which their newly acquired expertise could be used to benefit their homelands upon their return from America. But such is not the case. It turns out that the most crowded field of study for foreign students is Engineering (19.3%), followed closely by 18.1% taking courses in Business.

Other areas attracting large numbers of foreigners include Computer and Information Sciences (5.4%), Social Sciences (4.8%), Physical Sciences (4.6%), English Language (4%) and Liberal and General Studies (2.9%). Some 25,580 students (7.6% of the total) have their field of study listed as "undeclared" in the survey.

Agricultural studies attracted only 2.5% of the foreign students, a curiously small number considering all the talk heard daily about starvation in the Third World. One would think that more foreign students coming from hungry countries would want to help feed their people -- if, that is, they planned ever to return. Instead, most foreign students seem interested in studying those subjects that will help them get ahead personally in the United States, as if they never intend to return home.

On this point, Crewdson observes: "The real concern, however, is the significant numbers of foreign students who stay in this country illegally after they are graduated."

Crewdson notes that it is often not necessary for a foreign national to be admitted to study at an American school in order to obtain the I-20 student visa immigration permit. Says Crewdson, "Even though the forms are supposed to be issued only after a student has been accepted, in their eagerness to attract paying students, colleges often give recruiters stacks of pre-signed I-20s to pass out to prospective candidates overseas. The recruiters sell the students to the schools, receiving as much as 15 percent of the first year's tuition as their commission."

Many of the problems associated with the I-20 and student visas can be clearly traced to the schools themselves. While the issuing school is required by law to inform the INS when a foreign student graduates or stops attending classes, the schools, in an effort to maintain high enrollment figures to justify additional state and federal financial assistance, or through lack of administrative manpower, often neglect to inform the INS of a student's change in status.

For resident aliens -- those individuals qualifying for emigration to the U.S. to establish permanent residency and perhaps become a naturalized citizen -- the INS issues a special form of identification. Possession of either the older INS Form 151 Alien Registration Card (the "Green Card") or the newer INS Form 551 Alien Documentation, Identification and Telecommunications Card (ADIT for short) entitles the holder to obtain a valid Social Security card, be legally employed and to qualify for a variety of federal and state benefit programs. Either of these two documents -- which resident aliens are required by law to carry with them -- indicate the individual has legally entered the U.S. and registered with the State Department and the INS. This may not be true, however, as either document is easily reproducible by counterfeiters. A Green Card or ADIT card can be obtained in the many border towns of Mexico, where those wishing to emigrate illegally are told, "Fifty bucks will get you everything." Most importantly, many of the counterfeits are so good that many INS investigators and most law enforcement officials are unable to tell bogus cards from the genuine ones. Consequently, an illegal alien possessing one or the other can live within the United States with little fear of detection. The first and most widely held document is the INS Form 151, the Green Card, which was issued from 1946 through 1976, and bears the photograph of the alien. In its 30 years of issue, the INS produced no fewer than seventeen different versions of this document, each of which was valid at the same time. In many of the versions, the differences were so slight that it takes a highly trained INS employee to distinguish between them.

In 1977, to deal with the problem of counterfeiting Form 151, and in anticipation of computerizing its records, the INS began to issue a new document, the ADIT card. The major

improvement of this card was that it contained a coded
information strip on the back that could be read by an Optical
Character Reader (OCR), a device similar to those used by
supermarkets to read coded prices on items.

The ADIT card still is not the ultimate solution to the
problem of providing tamper-proof identification of aliens.
Even though the ADIT program was introduced in 1977, as
of 1984, only about a third of the 300 INS offices are on line
to the INS master computer. And, according to findings of
the Senate Committee on Governmental Affairs, the sup-
posedly ''secure'' means of encoding data on the card was
compromised in 1977, when the Mitre Corporation, a consultant to the INS on the development of the ADIT system,
published a report on the means of encryption it had devised.
The ADIT card has been effectively counterfeited, as an
admitted document forger told a group of startled Senators
during the congressional hearings.

Because the I-94, ADIT card and other documents are so
readily counterfeited and obtainable on the black market,
many illegal aliens live with little fear of being caught and
deported by the INS. Sometimes, however, to obtain employment or tie into the protective net of social services, one
further document is needed. This is SSA Form 702 -- the
Social Security card -- and its associated nine-digit number.

Because of its many uses, resident aliens and even alien
visitors are permitted to obtain Social Security cards. In the
case of non-resident aliens, the card is merely stamped with a
special legend, ''Not Valid For Employment,'' and is supposed to be used only for school identification, identification
for financial institutions and for drivers licenses. However,
employers rarely, if ever, ask to see someone's Social Security card. Thus even an alien with a card stamped ''Not Valid
For Employment'' can often report only the number to an
employer and obtain a job. And the Social Security Administration does not check reported numbers very closely.
Months, sometimes years may pass before SSA discovers
that an alien not permitted to work is doing so and using his

SSA number. What is more, SSA has a long history of being uncooperative with other governmental agencies, such as the INS, in reporting SSA number discrepancies and in bringing lawbreakers to justice. Even when the INS receives lists of aliens illegally working, the agency does not have the manpower to apprehend even a tiny fraction of the malefactors. More incredible is the fact that Social Security often pays benefits to illegally employed aliens, despite the fact that such aliens were violating the law in the first place. Untold millions of dollars in Social Security benefits are going to illegal aliens every year.

Americans work an average of 20.5 years before drawing Social Security. Aliens work only about 10.5 years. After this lesser pay-in, aliens receive about $23.10 for every dollar they put into the system.

Both illegal and legal aliens are looting the Social Security system. Senator Don Nickles (R-Oklahoma) spoke on the Senate floor about one legal alien who worked in the U.S. for several years, retired at age 62 and moved back to his native country. Social Security mailed his checks there. Once home, he began living with his own 15-year-old granddaughter in a common-law marriage relationship and fathered two children by the girl. This "family" received $12,896 in Social Security payments over a six-year period, and benefits for the children will continue until they reach age 18.

Unfortunately, a Social Security number, no matter how obtained, is also used by various state and local agencies as an identifier for food stamps and other welfare benefits, including school aid programs. Having obtained these cards illegally, aliens often avail themselves of these programs without contributing to them. Furthermore, aliens often use one legally obtained Social Security number to provide employment benefits to a multitude of other aliens. SSA investigators in Chicago told us of one number being used by several people to obtain food stamps, Supplemental Security Income and other benefits.

Another document which opens even more doors than

those issued by the State Department, INS and SSA and which is easily obtained by fraud or counterfeited, is the birth certificate. This simply shows that the individual in question was born in the United States and is thus entitled to all of the rights and privileges that go along with American citizenship. Since there is no national registry of births (or deaths), these certificates are quite easily obtained through local registrars' offices. Aliens, as well as common criminals, can assume a new identity by checking newspaper obituary columns, or even visiting graveyards and finding tombstones, noting the names of people who had been born at approximately the same time (so that their age would be believable) but had died in infancy. The criminal can then go to the county registrar's office and obtain a copy of the birth certificate of the person whose identity he wishes to assume.

Alien smugglers have hit upon this scheme. Some have gone the common criminal one better. Using a Texas law which allows for the back registry of births, a "document broker" can write to the Texas State Registrar stating that his "client" had been born in the United States of illegal alien parents some years before.

After a search of the files, the Texas officials send the "broker" the forms needed to file a "Delayed Certificate of Live Birth." This is then filled out and sent with accompanying "documentary" support (often an affidavit from the "parents" or "attending physician or midwife," skillfully produced by the broker or one of his agents). The excuse given for not having registered the child at birth is that the parents feared to reveal their alien status to authorities. The various documents are then presented to the state, along with a registration fee of $2.00. The documents are regularly accepted at face value with no check of authenticity and so an untold number of illegal aliens have obtained Texas registration in this manner.

As John Crewdson points out in *The Tarnished Door,* in discussing "Oscar," one such broker, "the state registrar created a record of the client's birth and, ever helpful, even sent a copy to the clerk of the county in which the birth was claimed. All that remained was for Oscar's client to ask the county clerk for a copy of "his" U.S. birth certificate and -- *Presto! -- another instant citizen who could vote, hold public office, collect welfare, and perhaps most important, bring his or her spouse into the country legally as a permanent resident alien."* (emphasis added)

Once an illegal alien has a U.S. birth certificate, he is virtually immune from discovery. For example, in order to obtain a valid Social Security card one must report to an SSA district office and present some documentation of citizenship. The document preferred is a birth certificate. If the individual in question is disabled and unable to work, he can qualify for Supplemental Security Income (SSI), Medicare, food stamps, Aid to Families with Dependent Children and a host of other programs. And the alien obtaining all of these benefits may not have ever paid one cent into the system!

We do not know how much of this particular form of birth certificate fraud exists. In the case cited by Crewdson, "Oscar" charged $1,000 per client for his services and "when the FBI grabbed Oscar, it found ledgers in the trunk of his Cadillac showing he had taken in $232,000 during the preceding three months." And since there are over 10 million duplicate birth certificates issued annually throughout the United States, it is not surprising that, as Crewdson points out, "the INS thinks it will never be able to track down the thousand or so Mexicans Oscar turned into Americans, nor does it have the faintest idea how many other 'Oscars' are still operating along the Mexican border."

The use of counterfeit or fraudulently obtained identification by aliens to enter and remain in this country is, regrettably, only one part of the problem. As mentioned earlier, the documents enable aliens to avail themselves of employment opportunities, Social Security benefits and other public assistance programs -- the so-called "safety net" -- that had their birth during the "New Deal" and the "Great Society." It is true that the investigative and enforcement divisions of the State Department, Health and Human Services (Social Security Administration), Agriculture (food stamps) and the Justice Department (INS) do catch a number of the most flagrant violators. However, the relations and communications between these agencies are often poor to nonexistent. Thus, while an illegal alien may be caught, convicted of violating the law and deported to his country of origin, the same individual is often able to return to the U.S. (again using fake identity papers) within a very short time (sometimes just a few days after arriving in his native country). Security in the U.S. is so loose, the potential rewards so great and the potential punishment so minimal that it is certainly worth the risk to try to enter America once more.

One such case illustrates this problem. A Nigerian "student" by the name of James Aho Oseme entered the U.S. in 1976. For four years he studied in the Denver area and worked in violation of his student visa, including a job with the Colorado Office of Unemployment. In 1980 he attempted to change his student status to resident alien through an "arranged marriage of convenience" to an American citizen. The young lady became disenchanted with the arrangement and reported the scam to the INS. When confronted with the evidence, Oseme, who was at that time collecting unemployment benefits illegally, agreed to leave the U.S. voluntarily. He returned to his native Nigeria, then proceeded to Ghana, where he obtained a new Nigerian passport. He then went to the U.S. embassy in Ghana and obtained a tourist visa in order to "visit" America (this despite the fact that his original passport carried a notation that he had left the U.S. under orders from the INS). Within six months he was back in the Denver area.

The Oseme saga does not end here. Upon his arrival in Denver he registered at no fewer than three area colleges as a "student visitor," claiming to the admissions officers of each school that he had sufficient means to support himself independently. He then went to the financial aid office of each school and claimed to be a needy resident alien. As such he received over $12,000 in student aid, including government-sponsored loans and grants. Not content with this amount of ill-gotten gains, Oseme again filed for and received unemployment benefits from the State of Colorado and filed income tax returns covering his previous stay in the U.S., for which he received over $1,500 in "earned income credits." Oseme's scams were uncovered quite by chance by an official at one of the colleges in which he was registered. He was reported to INS, which launched formal deportation proceedings against him, followed by a grand jury investigation of his student loan caper. Oseme was deported to Nigeria and one month later also indicted for mail fraud. However, Oseme's story may not be closed. Despite having been indicted for mail fraud and having been deported to Nigeria not once, but twice, the Senate Committee on Governmental Affairs was informed, "There is no record in either the INS's or the State Department's intelligence lookout system on James Oseme. He should be in Nigeria . . . but no one knows whether he has received a new visa and reentered the U.S."

The Oseme case is a prime example of the lack of communications between government agencies and even within individual agencies. Had the INS alerted the State Department when Oseme first departed the U.S. in 1980, he might not have been given a visa for his return trip. Had the INS's own internal data management system operated efficiently (as is possible in this day of computers), Oseme might well have been intercepted when he landed in the U.S. the second time.

Unfortunately, the Oseme case is by no means an isolated example of the breakdown of our current system.

Even charitable organizations have been used as "fronts" to distribute counterfeit immigration and Social Security documents. Perpetrators of such crimes seem to invent new wrinkles every day in response to preventive measures taken by various agencies.

Given the premise that documentation fraud costs American taxpayers millions, and quite likely billions of dollars each year, and that fraudulently obtained or counterfeited documents allow millions of illegal aliens to live and work in the U.S. without fear of detection and deportation, what can be done?

The Simpson-Mazzoli Immigration Reform legislation, which failed to pass the 98th Congress in 1984, provided penalties for employers who knowingly hire illegal aliens. New hires would, according to Simpson-Mazzoli, initially be required to present two forms of identification. Over a period of perhaps three years a new, secure form of "work identification" (verifiable through a call-in system to an agency such as Social Security) would be phased in.

Due to the extensive use of fraudulent documents, the first provision of the Simpson-Mazzoli bill would have allowed the problem to continue for a time. The phase-in time could be put to good use if and only if a concerted effort were made on the part of the government agencies concerned (Health and Human Services, the Agriculture Department, INS, Justice and State Departments) to work actively toward cooperation in not only developing but using a secure identification card system.

This system would work as follows: When a foreign national applied for a visa to visit the U.S. as a tourist or student, his name and other vital information would be encoded by the State Department and a computer record made. Upon entry into the U.S. the computer record would be accessed by an INS terminal. A machine-readable magnetic strip could be affixed to the visa or a code number used in the visa itself. The INS would then know the entrant's status. The data base could be accessed directly by Social Security, which could process a Social Security number for the individual as needed.

A work identification card could be made secure in the same way. Rather than a cheap card which can be easily counterfeited, Social Security cards would be plastic, similar to a credit card. While the card would have the Social

Security number printed on the front, the back would have a magnetic strip which could contain verifying data. Upon obtaining employment, the card holder would produce the card, and the card could then be taken to a district SSA office where the magnetic strip would be read and verified by a computer linked to SSA's Data Processing Center. The entire process would take just a few minutes and could be done by a secretary or other individual in a business's personnel department.

The cost could be defrayed by charging aliens fees for services they receive from U.S. government agencies. Phased in over a number of years, the card system would not significantly increase the administrative burden to Social Security. However, since the technology already exists, the costs of implementing such a system rapidly are not prohibitive.

The very suggestion that some form of secure identification is needed has already prompted some critics to raise the alarm about "Big Brotherism." From the Communist Party and professional "immigrant rights" lobbyists to some conservatives and libertarians who should know better, the "spectre of 1984" has been invoked. They ignore the fact that a more secure card would be used *only* for verification of employment, and nothing more! Since the Social Security number is already used as a de facto national identity number, the choice of this document is quite natural. Few genuine objections could be raised to having a prospective employee produce a Social Security card which could be validated for employment purposes in much the same way as credit cards are being validated at the present time.

A second criticism is that it would be too costly to implement such a system, requiring new technology. When asked about this concept, a computer expert with Social Security replied: "That is not a valid argument. The technology is there now. The computer space needed is available and the concept would require little more than several computer programs to be written and implemented." The same individual noted that a similar process could be used by the INS, State Department and other federal agencies to get control of U.S. points of entry. It would then be possible to deal with the flood of foreigners who regularly visit the United States each year without resorting to "police state" tactics, such as the requirement that all individuals carry identity papers to be produced upon police demand.

The problem of identification fraud is large and growing daily. If we are to come to grips with the many problems presented by illegal immigration, it is a situation which must be addressed with effective solutions and cooperation between both state and federal agencies. If we make it harder for aliens to enter the U.S. and disappear into our vast interior, and if we make it more difficult for these same aliens to obtain jobs or collect welfare using false identity documents, the flood of illegal aliens will slow to a trickle.

CHAPTER 9

Importing Unemployment

Over the past decade and a half, the United States has been plagued with high unemployment. At the end of 1984, the official national unemployment rate was over 7 percent. When "discouraged workers" (those who have practically given up trying to find gainful employment, but who want to work) are added, overall unemployment -- and underemployment -- is much higher, totaling almost 15 percent. Yet, during the 1970s, two million new jobs were created each year. Why then has the unemployment rate remained at historically high levels for so long? It turns out that half of the new jobs created in the past decade have been taken by aliens, both legal and illegal.

The detrimental impact that immigration is having on employment is not understood by many people. There are even those who argue that high levels of immigration, whether legal or illegal, have no real adverse effects. One who dismisses the significance of immigration for unemployment is Professor Julian Simon of the University of Maryland. This oft-quoted professor charged on a Washington, D.C., radio talk show in 1984 that "our country would be a lot better off if that number [of legal immigrants admitted per year] was not 475,000, but twice that or three times that or four times that.'' Simon holds the curious view that the more staggering our national problems are, the better off we will be. In the same broadcast, responding to a caller who noted that aliens were creating serious problems in California public schools, Simon remarked that ''what has generated the advancement of civilization or economic civilization has been to have more and bigger problems. And what we really need in the long run is to have more and bigger problems than we now have.'' It is likely that Simon will get his strange wish, because unless we get immigration firmly under control, our current unemployment rate of 7 to 10 percent may well double to nearly 20 percent within a very few years.

At a time of high unemployment, the United States has been importing record numbers of foreign workers, both legal and illegal aliens. Aliens come for jobs and better pay. Only a tiny minority are genuine refugees or those seeking political or religious asylum.

Two commonly held mistaken views about alien workers are, first, that they are mostly engaged in seasonal agricultural labor, and second, that they generally take jobs that American citizens will not perform.

Contrary to these popular notions, relatively few foreign workers are farmhands or dishwashers. Due to its very nature, it is often difficult to gain information about illegal immigrants in the U.S. workforce. But where it has been possible to obtain reliable data, the evidence points overwhelmingly to the conclusion that aliens frequently hold good jobs that American citizens would gladly fill. And aliens are often paid more than the minimum wage -- frequently as much as $9 or $10 an hour.

A 1979 San Diego County study discovered that between 13,000 and 25,000 illegal aliens were working in that area. Only about 8 percent of the aliens were working in agriculture. Most held jobs in manufacturing, construction, retailing and service industries. The same study found that many of the jobs held by illegal aliens were attractive to unemployed Americans, including 93 percent of the manufacturing jobs, 90 percent of the construction jobs, 71 percent of service jobs, 69 percent of retail jobs and 50 percent of agricultural jobs. At the time of the study, it was estimated that between 10,200 and 15,200 American workers were being displaced by illegal aliens in San Diego County.

The Urban Institute, in *The Fourth Wave* (1984), a study of the impact of Mexican immigration on conditions in the state of California, concluded that:

- The majority of recent immigrants to Southern California, both Mexicans and others, are illegal aliens.
- One-half of the recent immigrants to California settled in Los Angeles County.
- Around 645,000 new jobs were created in Los Angeles County between 1970 and 1980. Over two-thirds of these jobs were taken by recent immigrants.
- The presence of Mexican alien workers has reduced wages in low-skill occupations.
- State expenditures for public services used by Mexican aliens have not been offset by taxes paid by them.
- About the same number of illegal aliens arriving in Southern California during the 1980s can be expected to find work as was the case in the 1970s.

In April 1982, the INS conducted "Operation Jobs," a major effort that arrested thousands of illegal aliens on the job. Eighty-two plants in nine metropolitan areas were raided. In the Chicago area, for example, illegals were discovered holding jobs that paid from $4.82 to more than $10 an hour. Aliens arrested at a Chicago construction site were earning $16.78 an hour. Illegal aliens in Denver were found working on jobs paying over $12 an hour. The average hourly wage paid apprehended illegals in San Francisco was $5.19. "Operation Jobs" opened up some excellent jobs for unemployed American citizens and gave additional proof of the impact of illegal immigration on employment.

Studies of the employment of illegal aliens in Houston,

conducted by Rice University economist Donald Huddle, found that one-third of the workers in commercial construction in that city are illegal aliens, earning from $4.00 to $9.50 an hour -- or up to $20,000 annually. Dr. Huddle observed that "These wages debunk the commonly held notion that illegal aliens are taking only those jobs that American workers don't want because they are so lowly paid." Huddle added that these findings "imply that some American workers are being displaced, particularly Houston youths and minority youths, who, even in boomtown Houston, show jobless rates often exceeding 20 percent . . . . The social and economic implications of the penetration of the economy by undocumented workers is dramatic. If the sample proportions of illegal worker participation are projected onto city, state and national construction programs alone, we find that all male youths and minority youths, aged 16-24, could, in principle, have been removed from the rolls of the unemployed . . . and that adds up to more than one million U.S. workers who have been displaced." Huddle conservatively estimates "a payroll in construction going to illegals of more than $7 billion per year, nationally."

A 1984 INS survey found that a quarter of the employees in the Silicon Valley are illegal aliens. As Harold Ezell, the INS western regional commissioner, pointed out, "These are jobs that belong to U.S. citizens and permanent residents."

And last year Rep. Fortney Stark (D-California) discovered that over the last decade, the Social Security Administration issued "non-work" Social Security cards to some 1.2 million alien visitors who knew the cards could not be legally used to secure employment. The cards were issued so that the aliens, many of them tourists and students, could make investments, open bank accounts and pursue other activities for which such identification is required. However, wages for work have been reported on nearly half of these cards.

"In other words," Stark noted, "over 545,000 aliens have taken jobs that should have gone to American workers."

Stark also learned that the Social Security Administration provides an annual list of names, addresses and employers of aliens who are illegally working to the INS. But the INS has not been able to use this "gold mine of data on alien law-breakers," Stark explained, because it lacks manpower and other resources needed to cope with the situation.

Professor Donald Huddle has been studying the involvement of illegal aliens in the U.S. economy for years. His research led him to conclude that illegal aliens displace American workers at a ratio of 10 to 6.5. In other words, on average, 100 working illegal aliens will displace 65 citizens in the workforce.

Those most hurt by the employment of illegal aliens are youth in general and minorities in particular. Barry Chiswick, a University of Illinois at Chicago economics professor, has pointed out that illegal aliens "are more likely to raise unemployment because of downward wage rigidity for low-skilled workers (e.g., due to the minimum wage), widen wage differentials and increase the use of income transfers [welfare] by the low-income native population."

Chiswick's conclusions have been seconded by Cornell University economist Vernon Briggs. On the basis of his research on the impact of illegals on the labor market, Briggs concludes that, "In the local labor markets where illegal aliens are present, *all* low-income workers are hurt. Anyone seriously concerned with the working poor of the nation must include an end to illegal immigration as part of any national program of improved economic opportunities." Because illegal aliens most often displace unskilled workers, many politicians and academicians ignore the problem. As Professor Briggs observes, "If illegal immigrants were coming into white-collar occupations -- lawyers, doctors, journalists -- this issue would be solved immediately."

Ray Marshall, a former Secretary of Labor and now Professor of Economics and Public Affairs at the University of Texas, has been arguing for years that the massive presence of illegal aliens from Mexico and other Third World nations makes it virtually impossible to bring down American unemployment rates to low levels. In 1980, while he was Secretary of Labor, Marshall estimated that if all illegal aliens were removed from the workforce, the national unemployment rate would drop to 4 percent.

There are a number of reasons why many employers like to hire illegal aliens. Illegal aliens are docile, since they work in fear of detection. They regularly accept working conditions that are unsafe and are often not covered by accident insurance. Even when illegal alien workers are paid more than the minimum wage, as they often are, employers like to hire illegals because they can keep them "off the books" and avoid withholding income taxes, Social Security contributions, unemployment insurance and workman's compensation. Illegals often work more than 40 hours a week, but rarely receive overtime pay, another saving to employers.

Even in more skilled occupations, employers often prefer to hire aliens because they will work for less than competitive salaries. Aliens can legally work in the United States if an employer will testify that an alien will fill a job for which no American citizens are available. Many engineering and accounting jobs are going to aliens, who gladly work for thousands of dollars less than Americans in exchange for the right to remain in our country. Calvin Trillin, writing in *The New Yorker* (May 28, 1984), revealed how immigration lawyers assist employers in conducting such scams. In order to be employed at a job the Labor Department certifies is not sought after by any American with equivalent qualifications, job descriptions are concocted that are not likely to attract citizens. This might include a knowledge of a foreign language, such as Spanish, that is not actually needed for the job, but which will scare away other potential employees. In many American colleges and universities, departments of mathematics, business and engineering are filling up with aliens who are willing to work here for much less than such educational institutions would have to pay citizens in order to attract them to faculties.

It is not unheard-of for a factory owner-manager to lay off his American workers, cut wages and hire a new workforce of illegal aliens. Businesses that use a lot of alien labor have a competitive edge over firms that employ Americans at higher wages. People in construction told one of the authors that they are being under-bid for project proposals by other companies employing illegals. It is now a common practice for employers to ask their illegal employees to call for their friends living in Mexico when additional workers are needed. Studies by Professor Huddle and others have discovered that many job openings are never reported to state employment services or advertised in local newspapers, as they are instead circulated by word of mouth through the illegal alien underworld.

This problem is becoming more and more widespread. Richard Slawson, business manager of Local 250, United Association Pipefitters Union, Los Angeles, informed members of Congress of such a case in 1984:

> As an example of what is happening, I can relate to you a recent situation that occurred with a construction company, Brown & Root, on a three-week project at a Texaco refinery in Wilmington, California. One member of this Union had met with an individual from Mexico in a restaurant in the area. Our member, who happens to be a Mexican-American, was told by the Mexican national that he had worked for Brown & Root in Mexico and had been told that if he could get to the United States they would give him a job as a pipefitter. He had then crossed the border illegally and was working for Brown & Root. This is a small example of the jobs that are daily being taken by illegal aliens and at wage rates between $15 and $30 per hour.

In Denver, Colorado, 43 illegal aliens were discovered repairing storm-damaged roofs, earning up to $100 a day at jobs that more than 430 Coloradans had applied for through the state employment service. And the *Christian Science Monitor* (Dec. 19, 1984) reported on a number of companies that purposely hire illegals, including "a southern California electronics firm that advertises jobs for computer assemblers. Callers who respond to the ad in English are turned away, but those who speak Spanish are told to come straight to the plant." According to the California Department of Industrial Relations, 81 percent of the 115,000 garment workers and 75 percent of the nearly 200,000 restaurant workers in Los Angeles County are illegal aliens. The *Washington Post* (Jan. 5, 1985), reported that about half the workers in Washington, D.C., restaurants are Hispanics.

Defenders of liberal immigration policies often claim that the flood of aliens, legal and illegal, are creating new jobs for Americans. This is seldom the case because aliens with their own businesses prefer to hire other aliens. What is happening is that alien enclaves are being built in metropolitan areas across the United States. These areas act as magnets for more aliens. Local retail and service jobs are then filled by aliens, not English-speaking Americans. The *Washington Post* carried a story last year about Korean-born Suk Lim, who operates the J & L Sportswear Company in Alexandria, Virginia. Lim opened his business five years ago and has only Asian-born seamstresses working for him, "none of whom speaks English," according to the newspaper. Similar cases occur throughout the country.

The presence of millions of Third World workers in our economy also tends to discourage modernization of U.S. industries. Dr. Arthur Corwin, writing in the Duke University journal, *Law and Contemporary Problems* (vol. 45, no. 2, 1982), said, "most illegals seem to perform work of marginal economic value, as in taxi-driving, domestic service, car washes, hotels, restaurants, laundries, janitorial services, or in the secondary labor market as assembly-line workers or garment workers. Teenagers or machines could do much of this labor, or it could be done in satellite plants in Hong Kong, or in Mexico's border industrial zone."

The flood of cheap alien labor entering our country, far from boosting our economy, is hurting it both in the short and long run. Not only are Americans being displaced from jobs, but alien labor is keeping alive inefficient, labor-intensive production methods. Were it not for cheap foreign labor willing to work for low wages, U.S. agriculture would be even more mechanized than it is. Said Georges Fauriol of Georgetown University's Center for Strategic and International Studies, ''Any nation which wishes to compete in the international arena must have a well-trained and productive work force. One of the chief problems the United States faces is a work force trained for a number of tasks which are declining in demand, while at the same time new technologies and trading needs require different employment skills and knowledge. As entry-level jobs decrease, particularly as automation increases, the kind of jobs most attractive to immigrants, especially illegal immigrants, will not be available, further exacerbating the competition between and among entry-level jobseekers in American society.''

The lack of future need for low-skilled immigrant labor was underscored by Bruce Nussbaum in his book, *The World After Oil* (1983):

> Immigration strikes at the very soul of this nation . . . and the problem can only get worse as we move into the twenty-first century. For it is cold, hard, inescapable truth that the last thing America is going to need in the years ahead is a flood of unskilled labor. As techno-casualties mount, a growing number of de-skilled people will be moving into the unskilled-labor pool. At the same time, automation will eliminate a growing number of jobs. Hence a growing number of people, many of them furious at their new lower status in life, will be competing for a shrinking number of jobs.

Economists Wassily Leontief and Faye Duchin have arrived at a similar conclusion. In their study, *The Impacts of Automation on Employment, 1963-2000* (Institute for Economic Analysis, New York University, 1984), they predict that ''the intensive use of automation over the next twenty years will make it possible to conserve about 10% of the labor that would have been required to produce the same bills of goods in the absence of automation. The impacts are specific to different types of work and will involve a significant increase in professionals as a proportion of the labor force and a steep decline in the relative number of clerical workers.''

Contrary to the oft expressed view, alien labor does not come cheaply to the country at large. Aliens are displacing Americans in the workforce. Each unemployed American receives an average of $7,000 per year in unemployment and welfare benefits. Professor Huddle has pointed out that benefits paid to displaced American workers are costing taxpayers $25 to $30 billion annually. And it is impossible to place a price tag on the damage done to individuals and families affected by alien-induced unemployment.

Despite the fact that it is against the law, aliens are receiving unemployment benefits and welfare. The *Sacramento Bee* (Jan. 19, 1984) reported that ''William Kennedy, head of the Modesto office of California Rural Legal Assistance, a public interest law firm, contended that although federal law forbids illegal aliens from collecting unemployment benefits, the state has previously allowed it and some illegal aliens working in agriculture have drawn it for about eight years.'' In 1984, the state of California, in the wake of a lawsuit filed by CRLA, rescinded a directive of their State Employment Development Office, which had required non-citizens to prove they were legal residents of the United States. This measure had discouraged illegals from applying for unemployment benefits. The California Employment Development Office estimated that the lifting of this bar would cost taxpayers an additional $100 million a year in unemployment benefits paid to illegal aliens.

At the present time, U.S. employers can legally hire illegal immigrants and no law prevents illegals from taking jobs in this country. Congress created this loophole in 1952 to satisfy business interests. It is a felony for an ordinary citizen to smuggle in or harbor an illegal alien. But, thanks to this congressional loophole, greedy businessmen are free to hire illegal aliens -- even when they know the alien is here in violation of our laws.

If caught on the job, aliens may be officially deported or, more often, permitted to leave "voluntarily," and avoid the creation of a criminal record here that might be used to bar the alien's future legal entry. Employers who make a practice of hiring illegals just turn around and hire more of them. They often put pressure on local law enforcement officials and politicians to discourage them from strictly enforcing immigration and labor standards statutes.

A number of proposals have been offered to deal with aspects of this problem. Immigration reform legislation introduced in the 97th and 98th Congresses included employer sanctions, intended to penalize employers who knowingly hire illegal aliens. Eugene Fitzpatrick, INS director in Phoenix, explains that "employer sanctions will get rid of the magnet for aliens crossing the border illegally."

Professional advocates of lax immigration policies, as well as some business groups and others who should know better, have cried that employer sanctions will discriminate against "foreign-looking" citizens and place costly burdens on over-regulated businessmen. This is nonsense. Employer sanctions proposals have recommended that *all* new employees provide documentation showing their citizenship or legal status, such as a new, tamper-resistant Social Security card. The employer could then call a toll-free phone number to determine that the document was valid and that it had been issued to the person using it. Merchants already go through a similar process to verify credit cards. This saves the business community and consumers millions of dollars every year. A like procedure for employee verification could lead to significant reductions in welfare and unemployment costs in the future, as illegal aliens would be removed from the workforce. Since all new employees would have to provide documentation, it would not be possible to discriminate against citizens of foreign descent. The only people who would be at risk would be illegal aliens seeking jobs and employers, who could face fines and jail sentences for hiring them. Such a law would actually end the much more serious problem of discrimination against American citizens by greedy employers who prefer to hire illegal aliens.

Incredibly, in the fall of 1984, Rep. Barney Frank (D-Massachusetts) introduced an amendment to the immigration bill then under debate, which would have made it illegal for employers to insist on hiring only American citizens. Had it passed, the Frank Amendment would have created a special Justice Department unit to investigate and prosecute employers who "discriminated" against aliens. American businessmen who wanted to employ Americans would be prosecuted by the federal government as criminals!

A number of states already have laws on the books outlawing the employment of illegal aliens. Unfortunately, these laws are rarely enforced. In view of the seriousness of this problem, these laws should be enforced where they exist. In January 1985, Colorado State Senator Steve Durham introduced legislation making it illegal for employers to hire illegal aliens. Durham estimates that as many as 90,000 illegals have been employed in his state at any one time and he introduced the state employer sanctions bill because he was tired of waiting for Congress to act. The bill was killed in committee because of pressure from powerful agricultural interests, which value cheap labor more than the sanctity of America's borders.

"Operation Jobs" was highly successful in that it opened up several thousand jobs for U.S. citizens at very low cost -- $184 total outlay for each illegal alien worker apprehended and deported. This contrasts favorably with other federal jobs projects, such as the Comprehensive Employment and Training Act (CETA) program and the Work Incentive Program (WIN), which provided (often only temporary) employment at an average cost of about $5,000 per job created. This gives a cost effectiveness advantage of more than 27 to 1 for the "Operation Jobs" INS raids. Dr. Huddle recommends that an "Operation Jobs" program be expanded and operated year-round, which he feels would "conservatively yield a social benefit of 750,000 to 1 million jobs per year for U.S. citizens at a cost of only $150 million per year. The benefit to American taxpayers would be almost $4 billion a year in savings of unemployment insurance benefits and AFDC payments alone." Each million Americans employed at jobs previously held by aliens could be expected to earn well over $10 billion annually.

Concerning the displacement of Americans in better-pay-

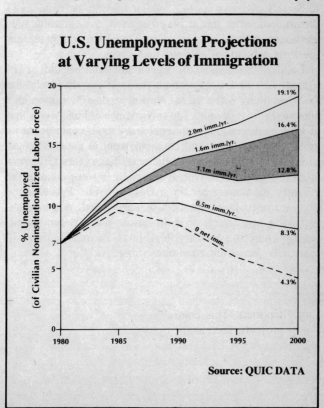

U.S. Unemployment Projections at Varying Levels of Immigration

% Unemployed (of Civilian Noninstitutionalized Labor Force)

2.0m imm./yr. — 19.1%
1.6m imm./yr. — 16.4%
1.1m imm./yr. — 12.8%
0.5m imm./yr. — 8.3%
0 net imm. — 4.3%

1980 1985 1990 1995 2000

Source: QUIC DATA

ing professional jobs, the American Engineering Association recommends that restrictions be placed on foreign students studying in the U.S., in view of the fact that so many of these students manage to stay here after their education is completed. AEA also suggests that foreign students should be allowed to study here only on an ''as available'' basis, with colleges not accepting foreign students ahead of American citizens; that foreign students be required to pay the total cost of their education, not the taxpayer-subsidized rate; that foreign students be barred from working while attending U.S. schools; and that all foreign students be required to return home after graduation. If enacted, these sensible suggestions would go far to curtail the illegal activities of foreign students, who too often abuse their status.

Finally, the number of legal immigrants should be reduced. Just to maintain employment at current levels, the U.S. economy will need to create more than 22 million jobs during the next decade. The Environmental Fund warns that if U.S. immigration, both legal and illegal, continues at its present levels, structural unemployment in the U.S. could rise to well over 19% within the next fifteen years. Given our high rate of unemployment, especially in some areas of the country and among certain groups, it is ridiculous to argue that we need large numbers of uneducated, non-English-speaking immigrants to help ensure our economic well-being. Quite the contrary; high levels of immigration will only make economic conditions worse.

CHAPTER 10

Aliens Raid the Welfare System

Defenders of liberal immigration policies often claim that aliens rarely use social services and actually contribute more in taxes than they receive in benefits. Recent evidence indicates that illegal aliens are making heavy and increasing use of tax-supported services, and often at higher rates than citizens do.

The additional costs to American society caused by aliens are especially evident in the areas of health, unemployment and educational services. For example:

• Nearly 80% of the infants born at the hospital nursery of the Los Angeles County - University of Southern California Medical Center are born to mothers who are illegal aliens.

• Los Angeles County's Health Services Department, with six public hospitals serving seven million residents, estimates that the annual cost of caring for the county's large population of illegal aliens is at least $150 million. The department reported in 1983 that illegal aliens represented 22.9% of the total patients and accounted for 64% of the births at county hospitals

• In 1983 the Arizona Hospital Association estimated that health care provided to illegal aliens in that state was costing $4.4 million, with the costs mounting annually.

• Nearly 10 percent of the population of El Salvador now lives in California. According to a State Department study, Salvadorans in Los Angeles are costing U.S. taxpayers at least $875 million a year. L.A. school board member Larry Gonzales reported that "the impact of the Salvadoran children on our public schools has been tremendous." And Los Angeles residents are being victimized by high incidences of communicable Third World diseases, which the Salvadorans are bringing into the U.S.

• In the state of Florida, following the massive influx of Cubans and Haitians, over $500 million annually has been spent by the state to meet the welfare demands of these unwelcome aliens.

• Illegal aliens in the state of Illinois have been taking millions of dollars in unemployment benefits to which they are not entitled. Spot checks conducted by order of Illinois Attorney General Tyrone Fahner revealed that 45% of the aliens who applied for jobless benefits were illegals.

• A check of 370 illegal aliens caught in New York revealed that they had received more than $500,000 in welfare payments.

• A pilot project, launched in Wisconsin in early 1985, identified 13 illegal aliens claiming welfare or unemployment benefits within the first few weeks, saving state taxpayers $34,000. Officials estimate that 10,000 illegals live in Wisconsin, and the program is designed to discourage them from attempting to make welfare claims.

• Thousands of Hispanic children are entering the Washington, D.C., school system, and $700,000 has been earmarked in the 1984-85 budget for special bilingual teachers. According to the District's director of bilingual education, "Some of the children have never been to school in their lives." Frequently, 12-year-olds arrive with the equivalent of a second-grade education. "They wouldn't understand an abstract idea like a fraction even if you explained it in Spanish," the official said.

• In Arlington County, Virginia, 26% of the students speak 40 different languages and nearly $2 million a year is required to run special English programs in the public schools. PTA meetings are divided into small groups conducted in Spanish, Cambodian, Laotian, Vietnamese or Arabic. And Third World hostilities have been imported to Virginia, forcing school officials to spend more on security to quell the outbreaks of violence between various ethnic groups.

Aliens are becoming so powerful in some parts of the United States that they are successfully pressuring local and state government agencies not to enforce laws prohibiting the giving of welfare to illegal aliens, and are further demanding that such agencies not cooperate with the Federal government. This problem is especially acute in the state of California, dubbed by *Time* magazine as our first "Third World" state.

In May 1984, city officials and police in San Jose declared that they would refuse to help federal immigration officials in their twice-a-week sweeps for illegals working in Silicon Valley. San Jose officials claimed that such raids, which have opened jobs to American citizens, are "discriminatory, inhumane and callous." On April 24, 1984, the San Jose City Council voted 9-2 in favor of a request that their local police, "to the extent legally possible," withhold any assistance to the INS in carrying out searches for illegal workers. The mayor of San Jose, Tom McEnery, went so far as to declare that "Although someone may be an illegal alien . . . . We want them to understand we're here to protect them. They should feel free to come to the police without fear we're part of the INS."

In late December 1983, the state of California's Employment Development Department implemented directives intended to make it tougher for illegal aliens to get unemployment insurance. The new directives required non-citizen applicants to provide documentation that they were legally entitled to work before they could receive the payments.

These new screening procedures were quickly met with lawsuits by the United Farm Workers Union and California Rural Legal Assistance. By February 1984, Governor George Deukmejian agreed to rescind the proof-of-eligibility requirements, thus permitting illegals to raid the taxpayers.

In November 1983, the Los Angeles County Department of Public and Social Services began implementing federal regulations requiring the reporting of illegal aliens to INS. This provoked loud protests on the part of Hispanic leaders, and "immigrant rights" legal activists, such as the Legal Aid Foundation of Los Angeles and the Mexican American Legal Defense and Educational Fund (MALDEF). Bowing to pressure from the Hispanic lobbyists, the county issued an administrative directive placing a moratorium on identifying and reporting illegals to the INS. According to the memorandum issued by Martin Woods, Director of the Bureau of Program Planning and Development, district staff would no longer identify illegal aliens, nor prepare reports for the INS. Welfare officials were not to advise applicants/recipients that they might be reported to the INS if they were in the U.S. illegally, and INS reporting posters were removed from welfare office reception lobbies and warning handouts were removed from the intake and recertification packets.

What has been taking place in California is now spreading to other sections of the country. On March 5, 1985, the City of Madison, Wisconsin, barred its employees, including the police, from cooperating with federal immigration authorities. Two days later, Chicago Mayor Harold Washington signed an executive order ending the city's practice of asking job and license applicants about their citizenship and halting cooperation by officials with federal immigration authorities. On April 8, the Cambridge, Massachusetts, city council voted to declare the city a "sanctuary" for Latin American "refugees" and cease cooperating with the INS. In addition, Cambridge extended educational and health services to illegals.

Regrettably, instead of enforcing immigration laws, the judiciary has often stepped in to extend welfare eligibility to illegal aliens. In September 1984, the Arizona State Supreme Court ruled that counties should reimburse hospitals for treating "resident [*sic*] illegal aliens." Justice Stanley G. Feldman, writing for the majority, posed the curious claim that illegal aliens can establish residency in Arizona by living in a county permanently without intending to seek a permanent home elsewhere. Thus, as county residents, they are entitled to health and other welfare benefits.

The California Court of Appeals ruled in 1984 that illegals are entitled to Medi-Cal benefits (the state's version of Medicaid) unless they are under a formal deportation order. California Deputy Attorney General John Klee said of the medical benefits that the court decision "seems to cover everything from aspirin to quadruple bypass surgery."

Following a lawsuit filed by MALDEF challenging an Illinois Department of Public Aid directive screening food stamp applicants, the U.S. District Court for the Northern District of Illinois granted a preliminary injunction ordering the IDPA to refrain from questioning household members about their immigrant status.

And in 1982, the U.S. Supreme Court, in a 5-4 decision, declared unconstitutional a Texas law which denied school district funds for the education of the children of illegal aliens. As columnist George Will remarked, "The court says, in effect, children who have no right to be in the State have a right to free public education."

Reflecting on the conditions outlined above, foreign affairs analyst Georgie Anne Geyer remarked that "Miami is no longer really the United States. Miami today is more correctly called the "capital of the Caribbean,' as border lines become fuzzy and peoples meld. The danger is that cities such as Miami -- and El Paso and San Diego and others -- will become simply social service centers for other peoples we have no responsibility for, yet cannot control."

Although alien advocates still claim that most immigrants

only come here to work, those who have dealt with recent immigrants know better. Sister Ann Wisda, who has worked closely with thousands of Third World ''refugees'' sponsored by the Catholic Church in Oklahoma, told the Lawton, Oklahoma, *Constitution,* ''Ninety percent of those who have arrived after the middle of 1978 have no intention of obtaining a job until they are forced to do so. The welfare mind has taken control of them and all they want to do is sponge off the American people.''

Economist Walter Williams, of George Mason University, has discussed the impact that the welfare state is having on the attitudes of our new immigrants. Writing in *The Arizona Republic* (July 11, 1984), Williams pointed out that ''When yesterday's immigrants migrated here we did not have a welfare state, and therefore we knew people would work when they got here: the alternative was starvation. Today, because of the welfare state, we cannot be so sure. People can come, not work, and live off the rest of us. We have too many American citizens doing that now; we don't need more.''

The public needs to become aware of the costly reality behind the myth that ''immigrants are a bargain, because they don't use many welfare services.'' Only after this dangerous fantasy is dispelled will it be possible to take corrective measures to deal with our worsening immigration problem.

CHAPTER 11

The Alien Crime Wave

One of the consequences of ceasing to enforce sensible immigration controls has been the wave of alien-related crime that has struck our nation from coast to coast. Our immigration laws prohibit the entry of criminals and ex-convicts, the mentally ill, persons likely to become welfare charges, prostitutes and procurers and other undesirable individuals. Despite the intent of these laws, politicians have allowed thousands of dangerous criminals and perverts to enter our country.

The 1980 Cuban and Haitian invasion of southern Florida turned what was an alien crime *problem* into an alien crime *crisis*. After the Carter Administration made it clear that no action would be taken to halt the illegal flood of "refugees" from Mariel Harbor, Castro seized the opportunity to rid his island of some of the dregs of the Cuban population and proceeded to empty his prisons and insane asylums. As many as 40,000 hardcore criminals and sex deviates were welcomed by Jimmy Carter with "an open heart and open arms."

Bullets and knives were soon entering the hearts of other Americans, such as Lieutenant Jan Brinkers of the New York

City Housing Police, murdered May 4, 1981, by Cuban "boat people." According to a shocking *New York* magazine article entitled "Los Bandidos Take the Town: Castro's Outcasts Shoot Up New York," some 2,000 Cuban gunmen prowl New York City, where they commit "thousands of shootings, robberies, and rapes."

"They seem to be the dregs of Cuban society, the sweepings of jails and streets," reports Lt. James McGowan of the New York Police Department. Most of the *bandidos* are followers of an African-derived cult and worship a "thunder god" named Chango; many are homosexuals. Their witches conduct a ceremony in which the blood of decapitated animals is dripped in front of images of their pagan gods. The carcasses are then burned and the ashes sprinkled on the *bandidos* to protect them from the police.

These Cuban *bandidos* specialize in armed robbery. If the victims show any sign of resistance, they are murdered. Among the thousands of crimes committed in the New York City area by these thugs have been:

● The murder of a rent collector in the Bronx by a *bandido* named Camacho, who strangled the man by tightening an electrical cord around his neck until he choked to death. Camacho was also responsible for strangling a woman and for raping another.

● A *bandido* by the name of Valdez, along with two accomplices, went on a crime spree, raping a woman in Teaneck, New Jersey, while her husband lay handcuffed on the bed. Another woman who was slow in handing over her purse was shot. Two days later, this same trio entered a store in the Bronx and shot and killed the owner, William Belin, and wounded his fifteen-year-old nephew.

● A man known as Lazaro committed several armed robberies in New York in order to raise money to go on a gambling trip to Las Vegas. After he lost most of his money, he began robbing stores in Las Vegas to pay for the trip back to New York.

● One man in Newark, New Jersey, sponsored 35 Marielitos and used them to form his own gang of criminal drug dealers.

• In a random act of violence, Ramon Carrelero murdered three bar patrons in the Bronx, calmly shooting each in the head.

The impact of immigration on just one New York City community is illustrated by a story published in the *New York Daily News* of December 26, 1983:

SLAYINGS: RULE AND EXCEPTION
by John Randazzo and Don Gentile

It is three square miles of the most murderous territory in this violent city. The Washington Heights section of upper Manhattan, where 350,000 people in the 34th Precinct are under protection of police from the Wadsworth Ave. station, has recorded 85 slayings this year -- tops in the city . . . .

To slow down the slaughter in an area where a bullet-riddled, slashed or battered body was turning up every three days at one point, police brass assigned more detectives and uniformed cops to patrol the area . . . .

"Did you know this area had but 10 to 12 homicides in the late 1960s and only one 30 years ago?" asked Lt. Arthur O'Connor, commander of the precinct's detective squad.

Since the late 1960s, "The Heights" has been changing from a lower-middle-class Jewish, Irish and Italian enclave of about 210,000 people to an area filled with immigrants from Central and South America and the Caribbean Islands. Many of them speak little English, and some avoid face-to-face confrontations with authorities under any circumstances. There are an estimated 150,000 illegal aliens living in The Heights.

About 70% of the 34th Precinct's homicides are drug-related.

New York City is "lucky": it has received only the "over-flow." Most of the Cuban criminals stayed in the Miami area. Within a year of their arrival, the Cuban and Haitian "refugees" helped turn Miami into the crime capital of the nation. After the last Mariel refugee arrived, violent crime in the Miami area jumped fifty percent. According to *U.S. News & World Report* for February 1, 1982, "Some authorities blame 'freedom flotilla' Cubans for almost half of Miami's killings last year." Sergeant Mike Gonzalez of Miami's homicide squad reported that,

> There has never been anything like it in our history. They are the most ruthless criminals I have seen in 31 years as a cop. Castro dumped his most hardcore, murderous animals on us, all at one time, and one place. Castro exported a crime wave that will be with us into the next generation.

Time magazine reported that "So many bodies now fill the Miami morgue that Dade County Medical Examiner Joe Davis has rented a refrigerated hamburger van to house the overflow." The *Washington Post* for December 22, 1981, revealed that "The jails are so packed with Cubans from the Mariel boatlift that Dade County finds itself in contempt of a federal court order to stop overcrowding."

The Cuban "refugee" crime wave has spread far beyond Miami and New York. The *Minneapolis Star* carried an interview with Thom Higgins, former coordinator of the Minneapolis Cuban Refugee Task Force, who revealed that, in many instances, refugees "used" their naive, altruistic sponsors.

In one case, a refugee stole jewelry from his first sponsor and, when he was placed with a second sponsor, had two friends come over to help him carry away most of that sponsor's possessions. "Several of the Cubans," he adds, "have joined gangs called *Juntos* -- small groups of men involved in bike theft, automobile theft and muggings."

Other communities in the interior of our country have suffered from the criminal activity of Cuban entrants. ABC Television's "World News Tonight" broadcast of March 15, 1982, reported that citizens in both Harrisburg, Pennsylvania, and Madison, Wisconsin, rated Cuban-caused crime as their Number One civil problem. Cuban criminals were found to be more prone to the use of violence --

especially shooting -- and tend to have no fear about the possibility of punishment. After all, as one police officer pointed out, American jails "seem like hotels" to the Caribbean criminals.

Some have argued that the alien crime wave will diminish in strength as time passes and these newcomers become "Americanized." The evidence points toward a different conclusion. Far from abating, criminal activity by 1980 Caribbean "boat people" is increasing in scale and sophistication. The New York Times of March 31, 1985, published a long report, "Cuban Refugee Crime Grows in U.S.," which pointed out that the "diplomatic agreement providing for the U.S. to deport back to Cuba 2,746 refugees classified as criminal or mentally ill offers little comfort to law-enforcement officials, who say that refugees who fled the port of Mariel in 1980 have been linked to an unusually large number of crimes."

Cuban crime is no longer limited to a few cities, but has taken on a national character. A Las Vegas police report concluded that "Our observations confirm a national conspiracy exists" among Cuban "refugee" criminals. A report prepared by the Harrisburg police on crimes perpetrated by Marielitos reveals the existence of Cuban networks conducting such crimes as airline ticket fraud, credit card fraud and cocaine and marijuana trafficking.

While officials of the Carter and Reagan Administrations still claim that only around 2,500 of the 125,000 Cuban "refugees" were criminals, the New York Times reports that "the estimate that appears most frequently in local police records and accounts by refugees themselves is 40,000." Refugees have testified that Cuban officials sent thousands of convicted criminals on the boatlift.

Local police officials complain that the federal government has shown little inclination to assist them in combating refugee-related crime. As Sergio Pereira, an assistant manager of Metro Dade County, Florida, complained, "Who let the criminals into this country? Washington." But federal officials have adopted the attitude that those who entered illegally from Cuba are "not our problem," Pereira points out.

Instead of expelling the Cubans and Haitians who arrived illegally in 1980, the politicians and the courts freed most of them from emergency compounds set up by the U.S. government. Those relatively few who have been kept in refugee camps, detention centers or federal prisons have shown their contempt for this country by repeatedly rioting.

Many hardcore Cuban criminals are currently housed at the Atlanta Federal Penitentiary. When CBS's *60 Minutes* program did a segment on these prisoners, one Cuban was asked why he was there. "I killed a man," he replied. "Why did you kill him?" the reporter asked. "He caught me stealing from him," said the Cuban. To him this seemed to be justification for the murder. And yet, the "public interest" lawyers who have attached themselves to the Cubans continue to file suit after suit in an effort to have these dangerous felons freed.

Even though section 241(a)(4) of the Immigration and Nationality Act makes aliens convicted of crimes subject to deportation, the Cuban and Haitian criminals and rioters are still here: politicians and "immigrant rights" lawyers have seen to it that our laws are not enforced.

The millions of illegal aliens flooding our country by land, sea and air clearly have little respect for our laws -- their very presence shows that. Many bring illegal drugs with them as they come. In 1979, INS officers seized nearly 53 tons of marijuana while arresting illegal aliens. Gangs of Mexicans have repeatedly attacked Border Patrol officers with rocks and guns near the border. The Border Patrol has been forced to obtain some special armored vans -- nicknamed "War Wagons" -- in which to conduct border watches.

Many illegals engage in crime as soon as they are across the border. Charles Perez, INS director from the El Paso, Texas, area, says half of that city's downtown crime is related to illegal immigration. In Houston, more than 30 percent of the city's murders involve illegal aliens. And Denver Police Chief Art Dill notes that illegals who cannot quickly find work "steal to survive."

In 1979, the Border Patrol located 12,449 aliens with previous criminal records. Mexican gangs have already made large sections of East Los Angeles unsafe for law-abiding Americans, and the problem is bound to get worse as more illegals enter southern California from Mexico. As the Urban Institute explains in its study, *The Fourth Wave: California's Newest Immigrants,* "Youth gangs unquestionably pose a problem. Since the mid-1970s violent gang warfare resulting from drug usage and dealing have become common in the barrios and public housing projects."

For over a decade, Cubans, Colombians and other Hispanics have played a leading role in America's drug trade. Billions of dollars in illicit drug profits have created an economic mini-boom in Miami. Drug dealers pay cash for condominiums, Mercedes-Benz automobiles, expensive jewelry and bribes to policemen. One drug dealer, Eduardo Orozco, came to the United States from Colombia in 1976, and over a four-year period used eleven U.S. banks and financial institutions to turn over more than $150 million in cash from his drug operations. According to a report in the *Washington Post* of March 14, 1984: "Colombia's narcotics trade is thought to generate as much as $30 billion in revenue a year for that country, whose foreign exchange surplus with the U.S. has risen from $405 million in 1975 to more than $3 billion."

Los Angeles and Denver are other centers for the drug trade, with Colorado Springs being a key transit point for cocaine trafficking.

Other "new immigrants" are taking advantage of our loosely enforced immigration laws: Japanese gangsters, members of a closely-knit, Mafia-like clan known as Yakuza, already heavily involved in prostitution and pornography rackets in Japan and Hawaii, have spread to California. Chinese gangs, manned by illegal aliens specializing in extortion, are today active in New York City, Boston, Miami and elsewhere. The *Jewish Press* of Brooklyn, New York, has reported on the "Israeli Mafia," composed of new immigrants from Israel whose criminal backgrounds are hidden from the American Embassy, which would not issue them visas if the truth were known. They have "continued their old ways," according to the *Jewish Press*, "preying on the Israeli immigrants first, and later, the Jewish community as a whole." A special report by the Israeli Knesset has revealed clear evidence of organized crime in Israel and direct connections to Israeli criminals in Chicago, New York, Miami and Los Angeles.

The problem posed by alien criminals is not new. From the early days of our Republic, foreign nations have often tried to dump their criminals here. Benjamin Franklin complained of this practice in an article entitled "On Sending Felons to America," published in the *Pennsylvania Gazette* in 1787.

In years past, our elected representatives passed laws to keep criminals out and then enforced those laws. Today the laws are still on the books, but our leaders have lost the will to enforce them. There is scarcely a community in America that has gone untouched by alien-related crime -- a crime-wave which will continue to worsen unless strong action is taken.

CHAPTER 12

Invitation to Terrorism and Subversion

Since the founding of the American Republic, a principal concern of federal immigration law has been the internal security of the United States. Indeed, one of the first congressional enactments in the immigration field gave the President authority to deport any alien he felt endangered the country's peace and safety. Internal security is still a major consideration, and current immigration law provides for the exclusion of certain categories of aliens from admission to this country. In practice, however, the immense increase in immigration in recent years, understaffing of the Immigration and Naturalization Service and rulings by liberal judges, undermine our ability to prevent dangerous aliens from entering the U.S. The erosion of internal security in the United States offers a perfect opportunity for hostile foreign elements to foment subversion and terrorism within our borders.

The Immigration and Nationality Act of 1952 (also known as the McCarran-Walter Act) remains the law of the land with respect to who may or may not enter the United States. At the time the law was passed, its major Senate sponsor, Pat

McCarran (D-Nevada), saw an urgent need for drastic changes in America's immigration policies. "Our present laws are shot through with weaknesses and loopholes," he warned. "Criminals, Communists and subversives are even now gaining admission into this country like water running through a sieve." Over thirty years later, his words still ring true.

The law requires the careful examination of all persons entering the United States. Communists and members of organizations affiliated with them were to be excluded. In 1977 the law was watered down by passage of the McGovern Amendment, which now requires the Secretary of State to recommend the automatic approval of visa applications of members of Communist organizations unless the State Department certifies to Congress that it would be contrary to America's national security interests to do so.

The intent of the McCarran-Walter Act has been further circumvented by the Refugee Relief Acts of 1953 and 1980, both of which have permitted large numbers of unscreened aliens to enter our country, despite warnings from security experts that many of the so-called refugees from the Soviet Union, its satellites and Third World countries are subversives or criminals.

Immigrants may arrive in the United States with unrealistic expectations about the level of affluence and personal freedom that they can enjoy here. The resulting frustrations lead some to form or join violent groups with revolutionary political programs. Such groups are easily manipulated by more sophisticated extremist organizations in this country, some of which act in concert with foreign powers. For example, perhaps the most serious terrorist act to take place in the United States in recent years was the robbery of a Brink's armored car of $1.6 million and the murder of three guards in Nyack, New York, in 1981 by the Weather Underground Organization and the Black Liberation Army. Another group closely linked with the terrorists in the Brink's robbery is a group called the May 19 Communist Organization. In 1979 this group issued this declaration supporting violence by immigrant and racial minority groups in the United States:

> Within the borders of the U.S., the struggles of the Black nation, the Native American nations and of the Chicano/ Mexicano people are building towards new levels of science, organization and power. It is this war of the oppressed and exploited peoples against imperialism that defines the terms, the direction and the timetable of proletarian revolution in this era.

In the same document the May 19 Communist Organization expressed support for the creation of a black republic in the southern United States -- a position also taken by the terrorist Republic of New Africa group, and Black Muslim leader Louis Farrakhan, a confidant of Jesse Jackson. May 19 supports Puerto Rican separatist and terrorist groups such as FALN (Armed Forces of National Liberation).

Speaking at a rally in support of the Nyack terrorists on November 15, 1981, Ricardo Romero, leftist head of the Chicano/Mexicano Commission of the MLN (Movement of National Liberation, a group linked with FALN), stated:

> We don't recognize the border. Our country was taken from us by the U.S. and the only way we can reclaim it is to wage war against the U.S.

Calls for Mexican-American "self-determination" and separation from the United States have become an increasingly popular theme among pro-immigration groups. At a National Chicano Immigration Conference, sponsored by the Committee on Chicano Rights, held at St. Rita's Church in San Diego, California, in May 1980, CCR organizers termed illegal aliens "part of the Chicano nation" and resolutions were passed calling for the abolition of the INS and the Border Patrol, for unrestricted immigration and for full rights to public services by anyone residing in the United States.

Many activists voiced support for the reunification of most of the southwestern U.S. with Mexico.

Among the radical groups represented at this conference were the La Raza Unida (The United Race) Party, the Brown Berets, the National Lawyers Guild (legal arm of the Communist Party, U.S.A. and very active in the "immigrant rights" movement), Socialist Workers Party, Communist Party, Marxist Leninist, and the Communist Workers Party. Among the speakers were representatives of the Denver Crusade for Justice, Prof. Rudy Acuna of California State University at Northridge, Dennis Banks of the American Indian Movement, and Father Alberto Gallegos of New Mexico, who praised the conference for reviving militancy and said, "we're organizing for battle."

Business Week for December 21, 1981, reported on "A Communist Push along the Mexico Border," and revealed that "A revitalized Mexican Communist Party, invigorated by a new, young, Cuban-trained and Soviet-schooled nucleus, is building an infrastructure in a group of towns on the Rio Grande along the Texas border . . . . With the border region's festering problems of high unemployment, illegal immigration and drugs, U.S. officialdom is concerned about the development of a local political movement with ties to Havana and Moscow." More recently, President Reagan's ambassador-at-large (now United Nations ambassador), General Vernon Walters, has warned that Cuba is trying to promote the secession of the southwestern United States, including all of Texas, New Mexico, Utah, Arizona, Nevada and California. Among Mexican-American "nationalists" this new Chicano "nation" is known as Aztlan.

The idea behind such rhetoric and activities is to politicize the unassimilated immigrant population in America and to organize terrorist and guerrilla groups from it to further speed the fragmentation of our country.

Lax border security and loopholes in official U.S. immigration policy have opened the possibility for foreign terrorists or their Soviet, Cuban, Libyan and Iranian allies to infiltrate this country. *New West* magazine suggested that there may be as many as 300 Palestinian terrorists in the United States. A group based in Washington, D.C., the Islamic Guerrillas of America, is led by and consists partly of immigrants from the Middle East who sympathize with the Ayatollah Khomeini and Colonel Muomar Qadaffi. It was this group that assassinated Ali Tabatabai in Bethesda, Maryland, in the summer of 1980.

Perhaps the most ambitious instance of the manipulation of immigration as a tool of foreign subversion is the use of the Cuban "refugees" of 1980 by Fidel Castro. Writing in *Human Events* for October 31, 1981, Latin American expert Daniel James reported:

> The 130,000 refugees who flooded into the country from the Cuban port of Mariel in April 1980 were essentially pawns in a plan conceived by Cuban President Fidel Castro and his intelligence service to destabilize the United States while relieving Cuba of "excess" population it could not support. The existence of "Plan Bravo," as it is called -- or Plan B -- was revealed in an interview with a recent defector from Cuba's General Intelligence Directorate -- or DGI -- named Genaro Perez. Perez operated under cover of a DGI-run travel agency in Miami, *Havanatur,* a front for fleecing Cuban-Americans visiting Cuba and recruiting intelligence agents among them.

According to Perez, Castro's plan was to seek U.S. recognition of Cuba by the Carter Administration. When this part -- "Plan Alpha" or Plan A -- failed, Castro sought to promote destabilization of the United States by releasing hordes of immigrants, among whom were hardcore criminals, sex deviates, mental defectives and more than 7,000 intelligence operatives and terrorists. Perez explained that Castro wanted to "unleash violence in the U.S. -- riots, disturbances, bombings, shootouts, assaults on banks -- in an effort to terrorize the American public and government." Puerto Rican terrorists, such as FALN, play a key role in this plan, which Perez says "involves incitement of racial conflict among Mexicans, Puerto Ricans and 'especially blacks.' " The CIA warned the Carter Administration of Castro's plan to unload the "refugees" four months before the boatlift began in April 1980.

Robert Moss, an internationally respected journalist and intelligence expert, testified before the Senate Subcommittee on Security and Terrorism on June 26, 1981, describing a secret meeting held by Castro in Nicaragua in July 1980. According to Moss:

> Castro boasted . . . that Cuba . . . had developed the capacity to ignite race war in the United States . . . claiming that "we can make the Miami upheavals look like a sunshower."

Robert Moss provided additional information on Castro's plans for the United States in an article published in the London *Daily Telegraph* of February 8, 1981. At discussions held in Havana on the "problems of minorities" in the United States, the Cuban propaganda line was that ethnic minorities such as blacks, Mexicans, Puerto Ricans, Cubans and American Indians "are subjected to constant exploitation and cruel discrimination." Cuban officials are contemplating staging another mass exodus of Cubans to southern Florida. Estimates of Cubans wanting to emigrate range from 400,000 to one million.

As the Cuban refugees spread throughout the United States, reports of their criminal activity started to appear. For example, the *Washington Post* for December 8, 1981, noted, "There is bitterness in the Bronx and in New York City regarding the flotilla these days. In the last year, according to police, there have been an estimated 1,000 arrests in New York City of Cubans who came to this country in the Mariel, Cuba-to-Key West boat flotilla."

Further evidence that Castro's plan to disrupt the United States has been making headway emerged with reports of Communist involvement in terrorist acts, such as this one reported by the Associated Press on March 29, 1982:

> MIAMI (AP) -- An informant who turned over two Soviet-made hand grenades to federal authorities says there are hundreds more in the Miami area, according to an FBI official. Authorities believe similar grenades were used in at least three bombings in the past 18 months in the Miami area. The informant, who was not identified, told investigators he saw at least 235 grenades hidden at a Miami home, FBI agent Jim Freeman said Saturday. An Air Force bomb expert identified the grenades as Soviet-made, Freeman said. The informant said he got the grenades from a suspected drug dealer he thought to be a Cuban agent who urged him to engage in terrorist bombings.

A related internal security threat arises from the presence of growing numbers of foreign students, businessmen and tourists in the United States. Such persons, especially those from hostile or unstable nations, are potential recruits by their governments for terrorism, covert action or espionage against our country. To cite just one example, soon after the Iranian seizure of the U.S. Embassy in Tehran in 1979, several Iranian students in the United States were arrested for attempting to assassinate the governor of Minnesota. Speaking before the Los Angeles World Affairs Council on December 18, 1981, Attorney General William French Smith described the increased threat of ''hostile intelligence'' activities within the United States:

> Although virtually non-existent prior to 1973, Soviet immigration here has since then amounted to some 150,000. More recently, there has been a vast influx of Cuban refugees -- who last year alone exceeded 100,000. We believe that a small but significant fraction of these recent refugees have been agents of Soviet and Cuban intelligence. Finally, we know that hostile intelligence services continue to infiltrate agents under assumed identities. In 1980 the FBI disclosed that Colonel Rudolph Hermann of the KGB had entered this country through Canada with his wife and son a dozen years

earlier and had thereafter posed as a freelance photographer
living in a suburb of New York City.

While the FBI tries to keep the "sleeper" agents under
surveillance, the problem posed by the new wave of Soviet
agents, smuggled in among the rising tide of refugees, is
straining government resources, as pointed out by *U.S. News
& World Report* for March 8, 1982: "Exact numbers are kept
secret on grounds of national security, but word on Capitol
Hill is that Congress will vote more money than requested for
the FBI to keep track of foreign intelligence agents in the
United States. Even the administration admits that a surge in
Soviet-bloc agents in Washington embassies, the United
Nations and among recent refugees from Russia and Cuba is
so big that the FBI can't keep tabs on them all."

Further evidence of the deadly seriousness of this problem
emerged with the arrest on October 2, 1984, of Russian
immigrants Nikolay and Svetlana Ogorodnikov, who entered
the United States in 1973 as Jewish refugees. They have been
charged by the FBI with conspiring to pay an FBI agent,
Richard Miller, for secret documents on American counter-
espionage activities. One document was passed by Miller to
the Ogorodnikovs, who turned it over to Soviet authorities.
The FBI reported that the document could give the KGB "a
detailed picture of FBI and U.S. intelligence activities, techniques and requirements." As the *New York Times* reported
on October 20, 1984, "The circumstances of the couple's
entry raise questions how well American security agencies
are able to scrutinize tens of thousands of Soviet emigrants,
mostly Jews and Armenians, who have come to the United
States since the late 1960s."

Even when terrorism and internal destabilization are not
coordinated by enemies like Castro, foreign terrorists sometimes seek refuge in the United States by illegally entering
our country. Once here, they may turn their violence against
Americans or try to mobilize support for their comrades
abroad. FBI Director William Webster has warned of the

grave danger posed by foreign groups carrying their quarrels and causes to this country -- groups such as those opposing the Philippine government, the Armenian terrorists who have conducted a number of attacks against Turkish officials in this country, Puerto Rican terrorists and anti-Castro Cuban terrorists. "Most of the terrorist activities," reports FBI Director Webster, "with the exception of Puerto Rico, have to do with people in the United States with causes that don't involve the United States."

It is clear that unrestricted immigration poses a serious threat to the internal security of the United States. Incidents of alien-related terrorism, subversion and criminal activity are on the rise and immigration analysts feel that we have only witnessed the beginning of the destabilizing impact of the recent wave of immigration. Failure to regain control of our borders and to police aliens once they cross into the interior of the country is contributing to a dangerous increase in the level of violence in this country and in growing opportunities for foreign subversion and espionage.

CHAPTER 13

The Alien Health Threat

One of the areas where the United States has progressed most certainly and most dramatically is in the control of disease. Swamps have been drained, sanitation has been improved and personal hygiene stressed, vaccines have been discovered -- all of which have contributed to the improvement of our public health to the point where many diseases that were once common here (and still are common elsewhere in the world) have all but vanished from the U.S.

The alien invasion of America is confronting our country with a new health threat. Diseases once practically eradicated are breaking out again. New diseases, previously unheard of in the United States but prevalent in Third World nations, are making their appearance here.

Historically, health standards for immigrants were rigidly enforced. Even today, under section 212 of the Immigration and Nationality Act (8 U.S. Code 1182), the Attorney General is not to admit aliens into the United States if they are afflicted with certain mental or physical conditions, any "dangerous contagious disease," or any defect, disease or disability that may affect their ability to earn a living. Public Health Service regulations define the dangerous contagious diseases to include infectious leprosy, active tuberculosis and venereal diseases.

A turning point in our government's policy toward the entry of aliens infected with contagious diseases came on March 15, 1980, when the Attorney General, acting on a request from the Secretary of State to expedite the processing of Indochinese refugees, decided to lower the health qualifications for admitting so-called refugees to our country. From this point on, refugees have been permitted to enter the United States who would earlier have been excluded, including people afflicted with active tuberculosis, mental retardation, previous attacks of insanity and infectious leprosy. No studies were conducted by the Surgeon General to ascertain the risk to public health presented by this change in policy.

Two days after the new guidelines were issued by the Attorney General, the Refugee Act of 1980 was enacted to amend the Immigration and Nationality Act. Among other things, it authorized the Attorney General to waive the statutory health requirements, subject to certain conditions. In April 1980, the State Department notified overseas posts handling Indochinese refugees of the revised medical processing criteria and directed that refugees be quickly processed.

An investigation by the General Accounting Office (GAO) Human Resources Division raised serious doubts about the federal government's procedures for screening foreigners with suspected health problems. The GAO was especially critical of the government's handling of refugees with possible cases of infectious tuberculosis.

The methods used to test refugees were superficial. Refugees were being permitted to enter the United States after just a cursory TB examination, and it was discovered only after their arrival on our shores that they were, in fact, carriers of the infectious disease.

It should not be forgotten that around the turn of the century, tuberculosis was the second leading cause of death in the United States. By 1980, its incidence had declined to 12 cases per 100,000 population. The U.S. Centers for

Disease Control reported that refugees who entered the U.S. in 1980, with no evidence of disease when screened overseas, had a reported TB rate of 407 cases per 100,000 population -- 34 times higher than the overall rate in the U.S. In total, the CDC found that Indochinese refugees had a reported rate of 1,138 cases of active TB per 100,000 population. Some Southeast Asian refugee camps reported TB rates as high as 10,000 cases per 100,000 population.

The Los Angeles County Medical Director reported that, in 1981, 41 percent of the refugees given tuberculosis skin tests reacted positively, compared to a 6 percent rate for American whites and a 14 percent rate for black citizens. However, the refugee skin reactions were lower than some other ethnic groups, such as Hispanics (including illegal aliens), who have a 50 percent positive reaction rate.

Prince George's County, Maryland, health officials have warned that it would take from three to five years to determine the full impact of tuberculosis in refugees. The future danger to our public health is clear.

As the GAO pointed out, "The high rates of tuberculosis in refugees are a concern because the disease can be spread to others." The Centers for Disease Control, in a study of refugees who arrived in 1979 and 1980, showed that:

• In the 4-and-under age group, the TB case rate in Indochinese refugees (439 per 100,000) was about 88 times greater than that in the U.S. population as a whole.

• In the 5 to 14 age group, the TB case rate (301 per 100,000) was about 215 times greater than that in the general U.S. population.

Tuberculosis is not the only infectious disease that aliens bring with them. Speaking before the House Judiciary Committee's Subcommittee on Immigration, Refugees and International Law, Edward Densmore, Deputy Director of the GAO's Human Resources Division, reported that:

Under the overseas medical screening process, refugees may enter the United States with other diseases and health problems that are not detected or not known to U.S. officials. In the case of venereal diseases, the blood test performed is designed to identify syphilis. If a blood test is positive, treatment is started in the Far East, but the treatment is not required to be completed before the refugee leaves for the United States. Also, except for a cursory visual inspection, no testing methods appear to be used for detecting other venereal diseases.

In the case of leprosy, the cursory nature of the visual inspection could, in our judgment, leave some cases of early leprosy undetected. *Some of the visual inspections we observed took as little as 5 seconds.* (emphasis added)

These procedures do not appear to be adequate to detect refugees with other contagious diseases, such as malaria, hepatitis or parasitic infections. In addition, the procedures may not identify refugees with problems such as mental illness, mental retardation (except mongolism), alcohol and drug addiction and many other major health defects, such as heart and kidney disease, diabetes and cancer, which could affect the ability of the refugee to earn a living.

In contrast to the lax health screening procedures followed by the U.S. government, the Canadians, who have also taken in large numbers of refugees, are stricter. The Canadian Department of Health and Welfare requires a more comprehensive examination, including a medical history, information concerning psychiatric problems and mental retardation, blood pressure reading, stethoscope examination and, in addition to the chest X-ray and blood test for syphilis, stool and urine examinations. Refugees with positive or suspicious X-rays will not be admitted to Canada until there has been a complete evaluation of the case and, if necessary, sufficient treatment until the disease is inactive. This process sometimes takes up to two years. Canadian officials report that some refugees rejected or delayed by Canada's process for admitting aliens immediately file for admission to the United States.

Overseas screening of refugees heading for the United States is clearly inadequate. So is the processing of refugees at U.S. ports of entry. Title II of the Immigration and Nationality Act states that aliens arriving at U.S. ports of entry are to be examined by at least one Public Health Service officer (a licensed physician) or a surgeon (with at least four years' experience) to determine if they have any physical or mental defect or disease. While the Refugee Act of 1980 did not authorize any deviation from the medical examination requirements in the Immigration and Nationality Act, in practice, the law is often ignored. The GAO discovered that aliens have been admitted in Honolulu, Los Angeles, Seattle and King County, Washington, among other places, where no physicians were stationed at ports of entry and where no aliens were examined for medical conditions or mental defects.

A further factor contributing to the spread of infectious diseases by aliens is that once they enter our country, they often quickly move from their initial place of settlement -- what is called "secondary migration." There is no federal system for tracking legal aliens after they leave their initial resettlement location. Aliens who have sought treatment for infectious diseases have been known to pick up and move elsewhere in the United States, acting as carriers for serious infections.

Unfortunately, diseased aliens have ample opportunities to spread their illnesses to the general population. According to David North, a leading expert on immigration and a former high official in the U.S. Labor Department, aliens (legal and illegal) are heavily employed in the food and beverage sector of the economy, such as in canneries, food processing, meat packaging, hotels, restaurants, bakeries, grocery stores and bars. Few states and municipalities require persons employed in food handling to be examined for parasites or other potentially infectious health problems before they begin working.

Quite aside from the danger presented to the public by the

THE ALIEN HEALTH THREAT   123

spread of alien-carried diseases, admitting thousands of
loosely screened refugees to the United States has strained
the resources of state and local health departments. Many of
the health services provided to refugees have not been paid
for by the federal government. And because of the high
disease rate among refugees, service to the general population has suffered in many areas of the country.

For example, from August 1979 to April 1981, Fairfax
County, Virginia, spent $270,000 to provide initial health
examinations, including immunizations, to refugees. During
this period the county received only $61,235 from the federal
government and Fairfax County taxpayers were forced to
absorb the rest. The Prince George's County, Maryland,
health department estimated that in 1980 it cost $238 to
screen and treat each refugee for communicable diseases.
The county received no reimbursement for these services.
This has also been the case in such places as the District of
Columbia, Los Angeles and Orange County, California, and
the State of Hawaii. The Texas Commissioner of Health has
complained that refugees have been brought to this country
by the federal government and then have been dumped on the
states and communities without prior clearance and without
proper health screening or adequate provision for compensat-
ing local governments for services provided to these aliens.
This has been especially trying when state and local budgets
are tight, at times necessitating cutbacks in services to American citizens to pay for the aliens' medical care.

Americans have worked hard since the founding of this
country to provide a clean, safe environment for themselves
and their families. All of that progress is being threatened
because federal officials refuse to enforce our immigration
laws, placing politics ahead of the health of the nation. The
most alarming consideration of all is that the outbreaks of
disease discussed here have occurred among *legal* immigrants who have been admitted in such large numbers that
proper health screening has not been possible. The millions
of *illegal* aliens who slip across the border each year receive

no health screening at all. Many carry infectious diseases and many are employed in restaurants in every large city in the United States. Unless swift action is taken, our nation is in danger of suffering from a public health calamity. The following is a sample of the reporting on this problem:

FLORIDA HOSPITAL
TRIES TO COPE WITH REFUGEES

Doctors and nurses at Jackson Memorial, Florida's largest public hospital, are learning voodoo, along with new languages and new cultures, as part of adjusting to care for refugees pouring into the state.

The often indigent refugees are also biting deep into the budget of the hospital, financed by Dade County [Miami].

"I've been here 10 years and over the last year the whole face of the hospital has changed," said Dr. Bernard Elser, head of the emergency room.

Overcrowding has reached a critical state at the 1,200-bed facility. Fire marshals recently ordered the hospital to find other quarters for 35 pregnant women, most of them Haitian refugees, lying on beds in hallways.

The cultural and language problems frustrate doctors, who must try to decipher patients' symptoms through translators. The hospital hired 20 translators in the last year, but doctors say they need 200.

Parasites and exotic diseases such as malaria, yaws and dengue fever are rife among the refugees, and tuberculosis is a serious threat. The rate of tuberculosis in Florida's population is 18.4 cases per 100,000 residents. The rate among Haitian refugees is 20 times that.

Natural illness is trouble enough, but some Haitians here subscribe to voodoo beliefs that blame angry gods for their sickness. "Sometimes we have to 'exorcise' them," Dr. Elser said.

Jackson has ties with an outpatient clinic that can put patients in touch with traditional voodoo healers.

New York Times
October 4, 1981

'NIGHTMARE DEATH' HITS 38 REFUGEES

Medical authorities said yesterday the mysterious deaths of 38 Indochinese refugees were caused by their hearts suddenly going "haywire" while they slept, but the triggering mechanism of the fatal attacks is still unknown.

The deaths of the refugees, some of whom died groaning in what is known as the "oriental nightmare death syndrome," have been under investigation for nearly a year by medical experts at the National Centers for Disease Control.

"Witnesses' interpreting the terminal groans in these (U.S.) deaths as signs of terror supported the popular notion that death resulted from terrifying dreams," or the "oriental nightmare death syndrome," the CDC said.

New York World
December 5-6, 1981

3rd WORLD IMMIGRANTS AND TB: SPREAD OF · LUNG DISEASE TRACED TO ASIANS AND LATINS

Los Angeles -- A massive influx of immigrants from Asia and Latin America has sharply increased the tuberculosis rate here and in other cities, a change so drastic it has reversed what was a steady decline in tuberculosis cases nationwide.

"The national steady decline in tuberculosis cases has stopped," said Dr. Laurence Farer, tuberculosis control director for the Centers for Disease Control in Atlanta. He estimated 1981 cases would total more than 28,000, a slight increase over 1980 despite a steady decline in the tuberculosis rate among most sections of the American-born population. Tuberculosis rates have also shot up in other cities with large numbers of immigrants, such as San Francisco, which is said to have the highest rate in the country at the moment. In the Washington area, public health nurses in Arlington County report they monitored 84 percent more cases of tuberculosis in 1981 than 1980 because of the heavy inflow of immigrants.

The Washington Post
January 4, 1982

LEPROSY RATE IN COUNTY
LAID TO IMMIGRATION

"I try to stay away from friends," she said. "Family is OK, but I don't want my friends to know. I feel ashamed."

At 31, soon to be a mother for the fourth time, she is pretty, friendly, charming -- and a victim of leprosy.

During the past two decades leprosy has increased more than 1,200 percent in Los Angeles County . . . .

Leprosy is a bacterial disease that attacks tissue, particularly skin and nervous tissue. Its more than 13-fold increase in the past 20 years is entirely due to immigration, said Dr. Thomas Rea, chief of dermatology at County-USC Medical Center and a professor of medicine at USC Medical School.

Los Angeles Times
October 14, 1983

EPIDEMIC FEARED VIA ALIENS' DISEASES

Communicable diseases carried by illegal immigrants from Latin America have some medical and health authorities in the nation's "new Ellis Island" fearing an epidemic.

More than 20 million meals a week are served in Los Angeles restaurants and fast-food outlets, and a University of California, San Diego, survey has found 42 percent of illegal immigrants work in service jobs.

Dr. Shirley Fannin, associate director of Communicable Disease Programs for Los Angeles County, said the immigrants have bypassed the routine pre-immigration health checks and "literally bring the diseases with them."

The most threatening to public health, officials say, are typhoid -- which can be transmitted in food handling -- and tuberculosis.

An estimated 1.5 million illegal immigrants from Mexico and Central America live in Los Angeles, which Rand Corporation demographer Kevin McCarthy calls "the new Ellis Island."

Los Angeles Daily News
February 20, 1984

CHAPTER 14

Amnesty: How NOT to Solve the Immigration Crisis

For years Congress has refused to grant the INS the funds required to enforce our immigration laws. As a consequence, millions of aliens have flooded into our country illegally, displacing Americans from jobs and adding to the strain on our over-burdened welfare system. But in the weird world of Washington, D.C., problems can be solved in some pretty odd ways. Many politicians have decided that the way to deal with illegal aliens is simply to make them legal by granting them "amnesty."

Some of the arguments for amnesty would be amusing if the subject were not so serious. One argument contends that the U.S. is to blame for not enforcing its immigration laws and not having a law prohibiting the hiring of illegal aliens (employer sanctions). Because "we" are to blame for not having enforced immigration laws, illegal aliens should not be punished if Congress finally does decide to enforce those laws. Persons who have entered illegally during a period of lax law enforcement thus deserve amnesty, or so the argument goes. This argument found favor among some members of President Jimmy Carter's Select Commission on Immigration and Refugee Policy.

Another argument raised in favor of granting amnesty to illegals (an argument that was also well received by Carter's Select Commission) is that such an amnesty would allow us to interrogate the former illegals and learn how they got here, making it easier to stop future illegal immigrants. In reality, immigration officers already know how illegal aliens get here and where they work and live, but lack the manpower to pick them up and send them home.

Certain groups which have long favored lax immigration policies, such as the liberal Lutheran Council in the USA, have called for legalizing aliens via a generous amnesty, charging that "enforcing the law by uprooting these people" might result in "infringement of the legal and constitutional rights" of "undocumented persons" (a favorite euphemism for illegal aliens). To these people, enforcing our immigration laws is somehow inhumane.

On more than one occasion the U.S. State Department has argued that Mexico would be upset if we deported their citizens who are in this country in violation of our laws. Some conservatives claim that deporting illegal aliens would disrupt businesses that currently depend upon illegal alien workers. Of course, there would be no sudden mass deportation of all illegal aliens if we started enforcing our immigration laws.

A favorite argument of "pragmatic" politicos on Capitol Hill is that we must give professional liberals, like Ted Kennedy, and Hispanic pressure groups, amnesty and other lenient immigration provisions in order to get *any* immigration reform legislation passed. A major flaw in that argument is that most pro-immigration politicians and special interests oppose *any* bill with effective employer sanctions, even if it has the amnesty provisions they want.

In many ways the most hollow contention is that the U.S. is unable to deport illegal aliens because there are too many of them here and we lack the resources to handle the job. This argument was made in the summer of 1984 by Senator Alan Simpson (R-Wyoming), a leading proponent of amnesty, who asked, "If we couldn't find these people when they were coming in, how do we find them now to get them out?"

As one Capitol Hill insider remarked in response to Simpson's argument, "The truth of the matter is that Congress has not even tried to stop the flood of illegal aliens pouring across our borders."

Every night Border Patrol officers watch helplessly as hundreds of illegal aliens who are sighted escape into the United States simply because there are not enough officers to catch them. Fewer than 500 Border Patrol officers guard our entire 2,000-mile southern border every night -- in the face of an illegal flow that now exceeds two million aliens per year. The authors talked to many Border Patrol officers, both retired and currently active. They told us that roughly doubling the pitifully small force to 5,000 to 6,000 would give them the manpower needed to stop the illegal flow across our borders. INS Investigators point out that they know where most illegals work, but, with fewer than 900 Investigators in the entire United States, they lack the manpower to arrest them. With adequate manpower and technical resources, we could deport millions of illegal aliens now in our country, just as we were able to in the mid-1950s. What is lacking is the determination on the part of political "leaders" to insure that sufficient funds are made available to enforce our immigration laws. One Washington veteran observed, "If our elected officials do not want our laws enforced, is it any wonder that our laws are flaunted by millions of foreign nationals?"

What is wrong with amnesty, which would "legalize" the status of millions of aliens now residing in our country illegally? First, it is wrong in principle because it would reward lawbreakers. When President Carter first proposed granting amnesty in 1977, then Senator from Pennsylvania Richard Schweiker pointed out that amnesty "puts the government squarely behind the lawbreaker, and in effect, says,

'Congratulations, you have successfully violated our laws and avoided detection -- here is your reward.' "

A generous amnesty was a key provision of the Simpson-Mazzoli Immigration Reform Act, which failed to gain full congressional approval in 1982 and 1984. Versions of this bill are being considered in Congress today.

During the 1984 debate on immigration reform, a strong case against amnesty was raised. William G. Hollingsworth, a professor of law at the University of Tulsa, Oklahoma, declared that any serious consideration of amnesty for illegal aliens must first await the U.S. government regaining control of its borders. Professor Hollingsworth warned that "A premature amnesty would encourage increased illegal entry. A nation so eager to grant unconditional amnesty before law prevails appears more than willing to extend it to those who arrive in the future. *It announces to the world that we are not serious about enforcing our immigration laws."* *(Los Angeles Times,* March 23, 1984, emphasis added).

This view is shared by Rep. Bill McCollum (R-Florida), who led the fight to have the amnesty provision of the 1984 Immigration Reform Act deleted. Rep. McCollum told his colleagues that "The passage of this immigration bill with the amnesty provisions in it will be a magnet that will encourage thousands, possibly millions more, to come across our border . . . in the belief that once we have given amnesty, we will give it again in a few years." And in a letter to his fellow Members of Congress, Rep. McCollum said, "Legalization rewards lawbreakers and is a slap in the face to those thousands of potential immigrants who have been waiting in line for years to enter this country legally."

Another opponent of amnesty, Rep. Thomas F. Lewis (R-Florida), challenged other Members of the House: "I pose this question to my colleagues. Is Congress prepared to take a stand against those who deliberately violate our laws? Those who prey upon our sense of sympathy and humaneness? . . . are we going to resist the temptation to let our borders disintegrate?" Congressman Lewis got his answer on June 20, 1984, when, by a vote of 195 to 233, the House refused to remove the amnesty provision from the Immigration Reform Act.

As Rep. McCollum and others had warned, as soon as the House voted its approval of amnesty, the Border Patrol could see an increase in attempts by aliens to enter the United States illegally. For instance, in the Chula Vista sector of California, the number of illegals arrested shot up from an average of 1,000 a night during the first three months of 1984, to between 1,500 and 2,000 a night within a month of the House's approval of amnesty. A spokesman for the INS told the *Washington Post* that "The word is out that Congress is likely to pass an immigration reform bill containing legalization provisions" (July 24, 1984).

Just *two days* after House passage of amnesty, Ron Chandler, Dallas, Texas, district director of the INS, reported that counterfeit document vendors were having "a field day." El Paso INS intelligence officer Joseph Aubin said that "amnesty kits" to prove U.S. residency were being sold in Mexico for as little as $75. On the Texas side of the border, "rent receipt books are big business. Even TV stores sell rent receipt books" used to document that a person has been living in the U.S. for two years, and thus is qualified to be amnestied *(Dallas Times Herald,* June 22, 1984).

Writing in the *Wall Street Journal,* Tom Bethell noted that

> The U.S. Catholic Conference will be involved in assisting amnesty applicants and can be expected to take an uncritical view of every applicant's claim; bear in mind that illegal aliens live in a world of forged documents, making their residency -- and hence their eligibility -- hard to determine . . . . The following outcome thus looms as a possibility. News of the amnesty will travel swiftly in Mexico and points south. The precedent of one amnesty will create expectations -- and pressure -- for another. Millions will head for the U.S. border, which, if the Hispanics and the Catholic Conference have anything to do with it, will remain as porous as ever. Perverse outcome: an "immigration reform" that results in

additional millions of undocumented aliens pouring into
America.

Amnesty for illegal aliens could result in adding tens of
millions of people to the U.S. population, over and above the
several million aliens who would be amnestied. This is
because, under present immigration law, aliens amnestied
would become permanent residents, who may apply for full
citizenship after five years. Once they become citizens, they
may bring in their immediate relatives -- husbands and
wives, children under the age of 18, and parents. They may
also petition for the admission of their brothers, sisters and
adult children. And after these additional people have been
here for five years, they, too, may bring in their relatives.

This process is known as "chain migration," and is likely
to bring millions more people into America by the year 2000
if amnesty becomes law. During the debates in Congress last
summer, Rep. Hal Daub (R-Nebraska), who was an immigration lawyer before being elected to the House, supported
McCollum's efforts to delete amnesty, saying, "The 'out-
numbers' [figures for relatives of newly legalized residents
allowed to settle in our country] are staggering and their
economic consequences suffocating to this goose we have
that lays the golden egg." According to Daub, each illegal
will bring in his immediate family, and these people will, in
turn, bring in their relatives. Daub told his colleagues that for
this reason the millions of illegals already here would be
multiplied sevenfold. (INS officers have estimated a multi-
plier factor of three.) Thus, amnesty would result in an influx
of tens of millions of foreigners, mostly Mexicans. As Ran-
dell Romine, a supervisory immigration examiner with the
San Diego district office of INS pointed out, "It'll be like a
snowball effect. The more legal registered aliens there are,
the more petitions will be filed . . . . It'll gain momentum
like a snowball, over a period of years" (Los Angeles Herald
Examiner, July 1, 1984).

Amnesty will also add to our bloated welfare rolls. Illegal

aliens already cost taxpayers hundreds of millions of dollars in welfare costs. Yet, many aliens hesitate to obtain welfare benefits for fear of being detected as illegal residents, and thus subject to deportation. Once amnestied, these people could obtain welfare benefits, including public education for their large families, without fear of any consequences.

The National Association of Counties sent a letter to each Senator and Congressman urging defeat of the Simpson-Mazzoli Immigration Act, warning that "the costs of the immigration bill [would be] $10 to $13 billion over a four-year implementation period, mainly because of social welfare benefits that would be made available to aliens granted legal status." The Texas Department of Human Resources told a staff member of the House Immigration Subcommittee that Texas would "not be able to support any efforts which increase the number of potentially eligible welfare recipients . . . . The State of Texas is adamantly opposed to any attempt at wholesale amnesty of illegal aliens currently in the United States." And the National Governors' Association warned that "legalizing the status of several million illegal aliens will increase state and local costs because legalized aliens will become eligible for forms of cash and medical assistance previously not available to them as illegal aliens."

Legalizing illegal aliens could cost Los Angeles County alone an additional $240 million, according to a report published in the *Los Angeles Herald Examiner* on July 11, 1984. L.A. County health officials estimate illegal aliens already cost the county $100 million every year. But, unlike emergency health care currently used by aliens, outright welfare is not legally available to them. Legalization via amnesty would change all of this.

Federal Budget Director David Stockman has estimated that amnesty would cost an additional $10 to $13 billion over its first four-year period, even with temporary limits on welfare benefits to amnestied aliens. But as Dr. Donald Huddle, professor of economics at Rice University and a specialist in United States and Latin American labor matters, points out, illegal aliens in this country already cost the American public $25 billion a year, and that cost will become permanent if legislation is adopted granting amnesty to those aliens. Huddle includes in his assessment of the estimated costs of amnesty the cost of unemployment compensation paid to American workers displaced by illegal aliens, the cost of social services provided to displaced American workers, and other expenses relating to the presence of aliens in the economy. Professor Huddle notes that "for every 100 illegal aliens working in the United States, 65 American workers lose their jobs." He estimates that 5.5 million illegal aliens were working in the United States by early 1984, displacing some 3.5 million Americans.

Since Hispanic minorities would be the chief beneficiaries of the proposed amnesty measures, it is worth recalling facts which suggest an established pattern of both U.S.-born and immigrant Hispanics on welfare. The Census Bureau found that counted Hispanics were 6.4 percent of the national population in 1980, and about 7 percent in 1982. But their rate of AFDC recipiency was 17% in 1982, and the food stamp rate was 15 percent.

This pattern of heavy welfare usage is evident. In Texas, Mexican-origin people were, according to the 1980 census, 21 percent of the population, but made up 40 percent of the AFDC recipients in 1982, and 51 percent of food stamp clients. In Colorado, Hispanics constituted 12 percent of the population and 40 percent of food stamp users in 1981, and in Denver, 21 percent of the population and 44 percent of the AFDC caseload.

In New Mexico, Hispanics were 47 percent of the population in 1980, and 65 to 80 percent of the social assistance caseload in 1981, depending on the program. In Arizona, counted Hispanics were 16 percent of the population in 1980, but 33.6 percent of the public welfare clientele.

In Los Angeles County, counted Hispanics made up 27 percent of the 1980 population, but were 33 percent of the AFDC cases, 44 percent of food stamp users, and accounted for 34 percent of Medi-Cal costs in 1982. In Santa Clara County, Hispanics formed 18 percent of the legal residents, but 38 percent of the AFDC clients, 37 percent of the food stamp recipients, and 28 percent of General Assistance users.

As a leading immigration expert, Dr. Arthur Corwin, points out, "Many public officials believe that the rapidly expanding Hispanic population could have potentially higher rates of social assistance than the current ratio." This is because, with amnesty, many welfare programs would, in time, become available to Mexicans who currently are working, but often at fairly low wages. Once they are "legalized," welfare, rather than work, will be a more attractive alternative. (See Corwin, *What's Wrong with Amnesty for Illegal Aliens?* AICF, 1984.)

Senator Alan Simpson, author of the Simpson-Mazzoli bill, claims that "Tax dollars will not pay for welfare benefits to newly legalized aliens for five years." He later said that amnesty would cost "only four billion dollars."

While a general amnesty for all illegal aliens has yet to become law, the Reagan Administration (after the 1984 election) permitted the INS to grant permanent resident status to the Cubans who illegally entered our country during the 1980 Mariel boatlift. Citing the Cuban Adjustment Act of 1966 as the authority for this action, Commissioner Alan Nelson said that the change of status applies only to Cuban nationals, their spouses and children, and does not benefit individuals from other nations.

This "mini-amnesty" was hailed by proponents as a great accomplishment, because Castro has said he will accept the return to Cuba of fewer than 3,000 hardcore criminals and mental defectives. However, in exchange, the U.S. agreed to allow the resumption of immigration from Cuba, despite the anti-American activities of the Castro regime, such as the illegal 1980 dumping of 125,000 Cubans on our shores. We are returning about 100 undesirables to Castro every month under this plan. In return, we will receive about 30,000 new Cuban immigrants every year. Also overlooked in this "bargain'' is the likelihood of Communist agents being infiltrated into the United States as ''refugees.''

This action is highly controversial and there is some question whether the INS has the authority to make such a move without an act of Congress. It should be remembered that once these more than 100,000 Cubans gain permanent resident status, they can then begin petitioning the government to bring in their relatives. Miami INS district director Perry Rivkind estimates that each Cuban will bring in an average of three relatives. Thus, through chain migration, amnesty for 100,000 Cuban boatpeople will really mean 400,000 or more Cubans on American soil, all stemming from the illegal acts of 1980.

Florida Governor Bob Graham did admit he was ''pleased that [some of] the criminals are going back.'' But he said that the state did not want to be saddled once more with enormous expenses created by an influx of Cubans. The 1980 Mariel boatlift cost Florida over $150 million. Increased costs in the areas of education, health care and police protection have become permanent and are continuing to escalate. An INS survey showed that Dade County (Miami) is giving as much as $8 million a year in food stamps -- 40 percent of the total county food stamp budget -- to illegal aliens (*Miami News,* Nov. 28, 1984).

Due to the recent waves of immigration, Miami now has a Hispanic majority constituting over 60 percent of the city's population. And it is no coincidence that the unhappy Florida city has replaced New York as the murder capital of the United States.

Clearly, amnesty is no solution to our immigration problems. As Senator John East (R-North Carolina) concluded,

> There is nothing inhumane in returning illegal aliens to their native lands . . . . Vociferous organizations which champion amnesty have also opposed employer sanctions, INS workplace raids, INS residential area control, and even replacing torn fences on our southern border. Before we give too much weight to their opinions, we should remember the

views of the majority of our citizens who oppose amnesty. In order to secure needed legislation to deal with illegal immigration, we should not have to offer amnesty to attempt to placate those who champion lawbreakers. Even if pressure groups fill the air with phony cries of "discrimination," we have a duty to enforce our laws . . . . Mass amnesty is detrimental to enforcement of our immigration laws and to the interests of the American people *(DAR Magazine,* March 1984).

CHAPTER 15

How to Control Immigration

Every poll has shown an overwhelming majority of American citizens agreeing that a concerted effort must be made to stop illegal immigration. On December 16, 1984, Dr. George Gallup released previously unpublished Gallup Poll data which "show the American public takes a hard line toward illegal aliens, with 75 percent favoring . . . a law that would make it illegal to employ a person who has entered the United States without proper papers."

Dr. Gallup found that "the public also strongly supports a proposal requiring all U.S. citizens and permanent resident aliens to carry an identification card." This would make it possible for prospective employers to distinguish illegal aliens from legal job seekers. The latest survey once again indicated majority opposition to amnesty for illegal aliens. The Gallup Poll results are similar to those of other polls conducted by such organizations as the Roper Poll, ABC News, *U.S. News & World Report, The Washington Post* and *Newsweek* magazine. As Burns Roper commented, "It is rare on any poll question to find such a lopsided result."

Polls further indicate that Americans favor reducing the number of legal immigrants admitted every year. While we may wish to continue to admit some immigrants, they should be from among the most talented segments of their respective societies, not the unskilled, marginally employable, as is the case with so many of the immigrants allowed into the United States today. Professor Garrett Hardin suggests that if we limited new citizens to those who are truly talented and who can enrich our country, the top limit might be 10,000 legal admissions per year. Others who have studied the impact of immigration on our population recommend that the number of new immigrants be equal to the number of Americans who emigrate each year. This would amount to around 100,000 per annum. And it has been suggested that we suspend *all* immigration for a period of three years in order to allow the INS time to concentrate all of its efforts on stopping illegal immigration, and then draw up legal immigration ceilings that will meet our needs. In any event, whatever the final figure for legal immigration, sharply reducing the number of aliens we permit to remain in our country will just bring the United States in line with other nations.

Writing in *National Geographic,* Griffin Smith, Jr. stated the problem simply: ''[The border] is easy to slip across; last year as many as three million may have done so.'' We must make it hard to slip across our border and hard to find a job -- or get on welfare -- for those who do get in. The challenge is how to achieve these goals.

Last spring, the American Immigration Control Foundation conducted a poll among veteran immigration officers and officials, both active and retired. They were invited to present their views on what steps should be taken to deal with our immigration problems. These men and women have hundreds of years of accumulated experience. Almost without exception they oppose amnesty for illegal aliens already here, support effective employer sanctions and call for additional manpower to help cope with the large number of immigrants, both legal and illegal.

In 1983 there were on duty an average of approximately 2,400 Border Patrolmen, 1,355 Inspectors and 760 Investigators. This is a fraction of the number of police officers protecting Chicago or New York City. In 1985, at any given hour, only 500 Border Patrol agents guard our entire 2,000-mile land border with Mexico. Despite these sparse numbers, the INS apprehends well over a million illegal aliens every year. As a matter of fact, during the first Reagan Administration, the number of illegal aliens apprehended increased 32 percent, even though the number of authorized INS positions decreased by 400. In the wake of the public outcry over illegal immigration and immigrant-related problems that cannot be ignored, in 1984 the Reagan Administration did propose increased staffing for the INS.

How much additional manpower would it take to help cope with our immigration crisis? According to the Border Patrol Supervisors Association, an increase from 2,400 Border Patrol positions to about 6,000, along with a corresponding increase in the number of vehicles and other equipment, could effectively secure our borders. The essential requirement is to establish a realistic deterrent: if illegals now slipping across our borders with Mexico and Canada, and through our ports, come to understand that entering our country illegally and then finding employment or obtaining welfare benefits is a long shot, then most of them will simply quit trying.

How much would this increase in Border Patrol strength cost? A rough estimate is less than $150 million. This is a very modest expense by government standards, especially when one considers that each million unemployed Americans cost taxpayers $7 billion in unemployment and other related benefits every year.

To apprehend the illegals already in our country, as well as those who could get by even a reinforced Border Patrol, and visa abusers who overstay their visas, more INS Criminal Investigators would be needed. The cost of tripling the number of these officers, along with equipment and support staff, would be under $40 million.

One way of paying for these new costs would be to impose

modest charges on aliens legally entering our country (both immigrants and non-immigrants). This could easily raise $200 million each year to help defray the cost of better enforcement of our immigration laws. Whether or not Congress decides to increase entry charges to foreigners, every dollar spent for effective enforcement of our immigration laws will be repaid a hundredfold in terms of reduced payments to unemployed American citizens, welfare benefits illegally obtained by aliens and other costs caused by illegal immigration.

Consideration should be given to closing the "citizen child" loophole. The number of "citizen children" born to Mexican visitors in U.S. border towns now runs as high as 20,000 per year. Tens of thousands of additional "citizen children" are born annually to alien mothers residing illegally in the United States.

"Citizen children" have legal access to nearly all U.S. welfare programs, such as food stamps and AFDC payments, as well as special programs for minorities, despite the fact that their parents are in this country illegally. On reaching the age of 21, the "citizen child" acquires the same immigration benefits as a naturalized citizen, including the right to bring in his parents, spouse and children from the mother country, with no wait or visa limits.

Such benefits help explain why the immigration of no-limit immediate relatives has risen steadily from 114,000 in 1976 to 143,000 in 1979 to over 155,000 in 1982.

Few other nations consider the children of illegal aliens to be citizens. In our case, this concept grew out of the Fourteenth Amendment to the Constitution, ratified in 1868 when the Reconstruction Congress was trying to protect newly emancipated slaves, not immigrants, from "Black Codes" in the states of the former Confederacy:

> All persons born or naturalized in the United States, and subject to the jurisdiction thereof, are citizens of the United States, and the State wherein they reside. (Amendment XIV, Section 1.)

Congress should pass legislation denying automatic citizenship for children born of alien parents temporarily or illegally in the United States. In any event, children born here to illegal aliens should have no right to bring in relatives.

Another abuse discussed previously is visa fraud. Thousands of aliens legally enter with valid visas and then stay beyond the expiration date or work without authorization. No one knows their exact number, though such cases have been estimated to run into the hundreds of thousands annually.

To help curtail visa abuse, Edwin Harwood, a visiting scholar at the Hoover Institution, recommends that an "abuser fee" be charged to incoming aliens. Writing in the *Wall Street Journal* of June 5, 1984, Harwood explained how such a system would work:

> Overseas aliens would post a bond collected by the airline [or ship company] at the time the alien purchases his ticket. The airlines [or other carriers] would handle the processing in exchange for the interest-free use of the money until its refund. If the alien is caught working or fails to return by the expiration date, the bond would be forfeited to the government.

The so-called "Sanctuary Movement" should be prosecuted vigorously for openly violating our immigration laws and endangering our national security. Since the spring of 1982, the Sanctuary Movement has operated an "Underground Railroad," sponsored by liberal American church congregations. Most of the aliens they have helped smuggle into our country have come from El Salvador, Nicaragua and other Central American countries. Leaders of this movement regularly attack policies intended to deal with Communist insurgency in that volatile part of the Western Hemisphere.

The Immigration and Nationality Act, Section 274, makes it a felony to willfully or knowingly encourage the entry of an illegal alien, or to transport, conceal, harbor or shield from detection an illegal entrant. Those guilty of such acts may be fined up to $2,000 or be imprisoned for up to five years for each alien involved. Tax-exempt status should be denied to all churches involved in the movement and U.S. citizens who participate in these activities should be prosecuted to the full extent of the law.

Another element of an effective war on illegal immigration is employer sanctions. It must be made a crime to hire an illegal alien knowingly. Although opinion polls taken on this issue indicate strong public support for such action, special interests have prevailed on Congress and prevented enactment of this sensible reform for more than a decade.

Opponents of employer sanctions claim that such regulations will lead to discrimination against any "foreign-looking" individual or person with a strange accent. Radical Hispanic politicians have conjured up the spectre of no future employment for people of obvious Hispanic descent. Some conservatives, anxious to maintain a flow of cheap alien labor, have claimed that employer sanctions will place "another layer of government" upon the backs of already overburdened businessmen.

Interestingly, opinion polls conducted among Hispanic-American citizens, though not their largely self-appointed leaders, show consistently strong support for employer sanctions, just as do surveys of black and white Americans. This is because Hispanic-American citizens know that illegals take jobs that would otherwise go to citizens, and that the many problems caused by illegals threaten to cast suspicion on the Hispanic community as a whole.

Contrary to the fears expressed by some conservatives and spokesmen for the business community, employer sanctions will not inconvenience anyone but the illegal aliens and the greedy businessmen who hire them. Nor will such laws discriminate against Hispanics.

What has been recommended is that a new counterfeit-proof Social Security card be issued to each citizen and legal resident alien permitted to work here. Upon applying for a new job, the prospective employee would present this card to the employer, who would then call an 800 telephone number to verify that this card belongs to this individual. Americans already carry a number of identification cards -- such as driver's licenses, credit and bank cards. The 800 number system is already working well to help curb credit card abuse. And this is done with little inconvenience to the businessmen or cardholder. While it is true that no card system is absolutely tamper proof, the microchip technology of today makes it possible to minimize the potential for counterfeiting.

Employers who intentionally violate the law should be faced with heavy fines and imprisonment for repeat offenders. The Reagan Administration has proposed civil, not criminal, penalties of $500 to $1,000 for businessmen knowingly hiring illegals. A $500 civil penalty is too small to be a proper deterrent. These fines would be considered just another cost of doing business. But if the employer and the personnel manager or job foreman faced being labeled as criminals, with the prospect of going to federal prison, very few illegal aliens would be hired.

Could honest businessmen accidentally violate such a law? No. As long as the employer verified the Social Security card via the 800 number, he could not be charged with knowingly hiring an illegal alien. The government would have to prove that the businessman *knew* the employee was illegal when he was hired.

Would employer sanctions encourage discrimination against American citizens who look or sound foreign? The answer again is no. The law would require that the employer ask *every* prospective employee for proof of his citizenship or legal residency, no matter what he looked or sounded like.

Some legislators have proposed that employers merely check two existing identification documents presented by potential employees. If they did that and kept a record, they could not be prosecuted, even if it later turned out that the documents were fraudulent and the employee an illegal alien. This proposal has been rightly criticized as ineffectual because of the large number of fraudulent identification documents available to illegals, and the difficulty of verifying the authenticity of documents currently in use. However, this system might be used for a year, while a more fraud-resistant system was phased in.

Reform is also needed in the treatment of so-called "refugees." Our experience with the Haitians who began landing in South Florida in 1980 and 1981 illustrates the problem. Although the State Department and the INS discovered, after careful investigation, that almost all of the Haitians were "economic refugees," not genuine political refugees, professional immigration lawyers have been able to prevent the deportation of these unwelcome invaders by requesting asylum hearings in the liberal federal courts. Such cases can drag on for years and, in the meantime, the aliens are here and often simply disappear into the festering alien districts found in so many metropolitan areas.

A streamlined hearing and appeal procedure is needed, and has been proposed by the Reagan Administration. In 1984, the U.S. Supreme Court ruled in an alien deportation case that aliens seeking to avoid deportation must prove "a clear probability" of persecution in their homeland before asylum can be granted.

Agribusiness interests have suggested that a temporary foreign worker ("guestworker") program might satisfy U.S. labor needs and reduce illegal immigration. Given our still high unemployment rate and the large numbers of Americans on welfare, it is doubtful that the U.S. really needs many more unskilled workers. Recent economic studies indicate that our over-generous welfare system discourages many people from obtaining useful employment. After all, who did these jobs twenty years ago? The whole idea that aliens are needed to do the dirty work is refuted by the case of Japan, which has almost no immigration, but has these needed tasks performed by its own citizens. Indeed, Japan's lack of immigration has promoted incredible productivity within a stable workforce.

Several European countries have instituted "guestwork-

er'' programs. These have backfired, resulting in the creation
of serious social, economic and political problems. Once
they are in a country, many ''guests'' do not want to leave
when the need for their services ends. The French government has offered handsome bonuses for leaving to guest-
workers who came to that country in past years. But due in
part to the turbulence of their homelands, as well as the
pleasant European environment, most of the aliens have been
reluctant to accept the ''leave'' payments. West Germany is
faced with similar problems from the large numbers of Turks
who came to that country.

Great Britain is also troubled with a stagnating economy.
Many British teenagers are unemployed, as are their American counterparts. Entry-level positions in Britain are often
taken by newcomers from the former British colonies. British governments, both Labour and Conservative, saw immigrants as a cheap source of labor for the inefficient industries nationalized after World War II. Now a number of
British cities have crime-infested, Third World neighborhoods, welfare abuse and job displacement of native Britons.
As in France, there have been increasing calls in Parliament
for programs to deport unwanted aliens. The European experience has shown that once people are in a country, it is
very difficult to get them out.

One simple reform that should be a part of new immigration control legislation would deny U.S. citizenship to any
alien who violates U.S. immigration laws. Foreigners who
have no respect for our laws should not be rewarded with
citizenship and the right to send for their relatives.

Even if all the reforms discussed in this chapter become
law and are vigorously enforced, the United States will still
be the most generous nation in the world when it comes to
admitting immigrants and refugees. Such reforms would also
go a long way toward protecting the future of the American
people, something many politicians have not worried about
for a long time.

What Can I Do?

You have already taken the first step by reading this book. An educated citizenry is essential to the survival of our free government. Now that you know how serious the immigration threat has become, you cannot be misled by the liberal media or politicians anxious to conceal their failure to enforce America's immigration laws.

The next step is to write both of your United States Senators and your Representative at the following addresses:

Senator _____
Senate Office Building
Washington, D.C. 20510

Congressman _____
House Office Building
Washington, D.C. 20515

Tell them what you think of runaway illegal immigration, of legal immigration that has exceeded 800,000 in a single year, of the idea of granting amnesty to millions of illegal aliens. If you don't express your views, the special interests, "immigrant rights" lawyers and others favoring the alien invasion will continue to get their way.

You should unite with other Americans to educate fellow citizens about this crucial issue. You can multiply your influence by giving this book to friends, relatives, neighbors, teachers, libraries, local newspaper, television and radio editors and commentators, and public officials. Use the order form on the next page to order extra copies of *The Immigration Time Bomb*.

You can also join the American Immigration Control Foundation. Your tax-deductible donation of $20 entitles you to full membership in AICF. As a member, you will receive copies of our latest publications, including our fact-filled newsletter, *Border Watch*. With your support, we can reach millions of our fellow citizens. Time is short and the battle lines are being drawn.

If we do not act now to reverse this invasion, the America we know and love will be destroyed, never to reappear. Our children and grandchildren will live and die in an overcrowded, poverty-stricken land torn by ethnic strife.

But, by working together, we can prevent that calamity. We can and must send the politicians a message they cannot ignore. Together, freedom-loving American citizens can save our country and pass it on to future generations -- stronger and freer than ever.

The choice is ours.

ORDER FORM

American Immigration Control Foundation (AICF)
P.O. Box 11839
Alexandria, Virginia 22312

Gentlemen:

☐ Please send me _____ copies of **The Immigration Time Bomb.** Payment of $_____ is enclosed (send check or money order payable to AICF). We pay postage and handling on all orders.

☐ Yes, I want to become a member of AICF. Enclosed is my tax-deductible donation of $20.00. I understand that I will receive your newsletter, **Border Watch,** plus other publications on the immigration crisis.

Name _____

Street _____

City _____

State, Zip _____

Prices for **The Immigration Time Bomb** sent to the same address. (We will be glad to send **The Immigration Time Bomb** directly to your friends at the rate of $2.50 per name.)

1 copy	$2.50
2-9 copies	$2.00 each
10-24 copies	$1.50 each
25-99 copies	$1.00 each
100 copies	50¢ each

About the Authors

G. Palmer Stacy III received his B.A. degree in History, *magna cum laude*, from West Virginia University and his J.D. degree, *cum laude*, from Duke University School of Law. After practicing law for several years, he became a top advisor to a leading conservative senator in 1981. Active in patriotic causes since the age of 16, Mr. Stacy is one of the founders and leading activists of the modern immigration control movement.

Wayne Lutton, Ph.D., is assistant to the president of The Summit, Manitou Springs, Colorado, and a consultant to the American Immigration Control Foundation. A native of Illinois, he attended Bradley University (B.A., International Studies), Colorado College, University of Tulsa, University of South Carolina and Southern Illinois University (Ph.D., History). Before joining The Summit, Dr. Lutton was a college professor, teaching courses on the history and politics of Modern Europe and Latin America. He has given a number of scholarly papers dealing with U.S.-Latin American relations and nationalist movements in the Third World, and is widely published in both academic journals and the popular press.